United States, Edward Wolcott

The National Bank Act

And Other Laws Relating to national banks, from the revised statutes of

the United States

United States, Edward Wolcott

The National Bank Act
And Other Laws Relating to national banks, from the revised statutes of the United States

ISBN/EAN: 9783337123567

Printed in Europe, USA, Canada, Australia, Japan

Cover: Foto ©Suzi / pixelio.de

More available books at **www.hansebooks.com**

NATIONAL BANK ACT,

AND OTHER

LAWS RELATING TO NATIONAL BANKS,

FROM THE

REVISED STATUTES OF THE UNITED STATES;

WITH

AMENDMENTS AND ADDITIONAL ACTS.

COMPILED BY EDWARD WOLCOTT,
UNDER THE DIRECTION OF THE COMPTROLLER OF THE CURRENCY.

WASHINGTON:
GOVERNMENT PRINTING OFFICE.
1882.

LIST OF LAWS

AND

PARTS OF LAWS CONTAINED IN THIS COMPILATIÓN.

TREASURY DEPARTMENT,
Document No. 314.
Comptroller of the Currency.

NATIONAL BANK ACT,

AND OTHER

LAWS RELATING TO NATIONAL BANKS.

CHAPTER ONE.

THE COMPTROLLER OF THE CURRENCY.

[The numbers in parentheses refer to the Revised Statutes.]

1. (SEC. 324.) There shall be in the Department of the Treasury a Bureau charged with the execution of all laws passed by Congress relating to the issue and regulation of a national currency secured by United States bonds; the chief officer of which Bureau shall be called the Comptroller of the Currency, and shall perform his duties under the general direction of the Secretary of the Treasury. Bureau of Comptroller of the Currency established.

2. (SEC. 325.) The Comptroller of the Currency shall be appointed by the President, on the recommendation of the Secretary of the Treasury, by and with the advice and consent of the Senate, and shall hold his office for the term of five years unless sooner removed by the President, upon reasons to be communicated by him to the Senate; and he shall be entitled to a salary of five thousand dollars a year. Comptroller of the Currency; appointment, term, of office, &c.

3. (SEC. 326.) The Comptroller of the Currency shall, within fifteen days from the time of notice of his appointment, take and subscribe the oath of office; and he shall give to the United States a bond in the penalty of one hundred thousand dollars, with not less than two responsible sureties, to be approved by the Secretary of the Treasury, conditioned for the faithful discharge of the duties of his office. Oath and bond of Comptroller.

4. (SEC. 327.) There shall be in the Bureau of the Comptroller of the Currency a Deputy Comptroller of the Currency, to be appointed by the Secretary, who shall be entitled to a salary of two thousand five hundred dollars a year, and who shall possess the power and perform the duties attached by Deputy Comptroller; appointment, duties, &c.

(5)

law to the office of Comptroller during a vacancy in the office or during the absence or inability of the Comptroller.

Oath and bond of Deputy. The Deputy Comptroller shall also take the oath of office prescribed by the Constitution and laws of the United States, and shall give a like bond in the penalty of fifty thousand dollars.

Clerks. 5. (SEC. 328.) The Comptroller of the Currency shall employ, from time to time, the necessary clerks, to be appointed and classified by the Secretary of the Treasury, to discharge such duties as the Comptroller shall direct.

Interest in national banks prohibited. 6. (SEC. 329.) It shall not be lawful for the Comptroller or the Deputy Comptroller of the Currency, either directly or indirectly, to be interested in any association issuing national currency under the laws of the United States.

Seal of office. 7. (SEC. 330.) The seal devised by the Comptroller of the Currency for his office, and approved by the Secretary of the Treasury, shall continue to be the seal of office of the **See act of Feb. 18, 1875, correcting Rev. Stat.** Comptroller, and may be renewed when necessary. A description of the seal, with an impression thereof, and a certificate of approval of the Secretary of the Treasury, shall be filed in the office of the Secretary of State.

Rooms, vaults, furniture, &c., for Bureau. 8. (SEC. 331.) There shall be assigned from time to time, to the Comptroller of the Currency, by the Secretary of the Treasury, suitable rooms in the Treasury building for conducting the business of the Currency Bureau, containing safe and secure fire-proof vaults, in which the Comptroller shall deposit and safely keep all the plates not necessarily in the possession of engravers or printers, and other valuable things belonging to his Department; and the Comptroller shall from time to time furnish the necessary furniture, stationery, fuel, lights, and other proper conveniences for the transaction of the business of his office.

Comptroller to examine banks in District of Columbia. 9. (SEC. 332.) The Comptroller of the Currency, in addition to the powers conferred upon him by law for the examination of national banks, is further authorized, whenever he may deem it useful, to cause examination to be made into the condition of any bank in the District of Columbia organized under act of Congress. The Comptroller, at his discretion, may report to Congress the results of such examination. The expense necessarily incurred in any such examination shall be paid out of any appropriation made by Congress for special bank examinations.

10. (SEC. 333.) The Comptroller of the Currency shall make an annual report to Congress, at the commencement of its session, exhibiting—

Annual report. See act of Feb. 18, 1875, correcting Rev. Stat.

First. A summary of the state and condition of every association from which reports have been received the preceding year, at the several dates to which such reports refer, with an abstract of the whole amount of banking capital returned by them, of the whole amount of their debts and liabilities, the amount of circulating notes outstanding, and the total amount of means and resources, specifying the amount of lawful money held by them at the times of their several returns, and such other information in relation to such associations as, in his judgment, may be useful.

Condition of national associations.

Second. A statement of the associations whose business has been closed during the year, with the amount of their circulation redeemed and the amount outstanding.

Closed associations.

Third. Any amendment to the laws relative to banking by which the system may be improved, and the security of the holders of its notes and other creditors may be increased.

Amendments to banking laws.

Fourth. A statement exhibiting under appropriate heads the resources and liabilities and condition of the banks, banking companies, and savings-banks organized under the laws of the several States and Territories; such information to be obtained by the Comptroller from the reports made by such banks, banking companies, and savings-banks to the legislatures or officers of the different States and Territories, and, where such reports cannot be obtained, the deficiency to be supplied from such other authentic sources as may be available.

Condition of State banks and savings-banks.

Fifth. The names and compensation of the clerks employed by him, and the whole amount of the expenses of the banking department during the year.

Clerks, and expenses of Bureau.

11. (SEC. 3811.) When the annual report of the Comptroller of the Currency upon the national banks and banks under State and Territorial laws is completed, or while it is in process of completion, if thereby the business may be sooner dispatched, the work of printing shall be commenced, under the superintendence of the Secretary, and the whole shall be printed and ready for delivery on or before the first day of December next after the close of the year to which the report relates.

When report may be printed. See act of Feb. 18, 1875, correcting Rev. Stat.

CHAPTER TWO.

ORGANIZATION AND POWERS OF NATIONAL BANKS.

Formation of national banking associations. 12. (SEC. 5133.) Associations for carrying on the business of banking under this Title may be formed by any number of natural persons, not less in any case than five. They Articles of association. shall enter into articles of association, which shall specify in general terms the object for which the association is formed, and may contain any other provisions, not inconsistent with law, which the association may see fit to adopt for the regulation of its business and the conduct of its affairs. These articles shall be signed by the persons uniting to form the association, and a copy of them shall be forwarded to the Comptroller of the Currency, to be filed and preserved in his office.

Organization certificate. 13. (SEC. 5134.) The persons uniting to form such an association shall, under their hands, make an organization certificate, which shall specifically state:

Name of association. First. The name assumed by such association; which name shall be subject to the approval of the Comptroller of the Currency.

Place of business. Second. The place where its operations of discount and deposit are to be carried on, designating the State, Territory, or district, and the particular county and city, town, or village.

Capital stock. Third. The amount of capital stock and the number of shares into which the same is to be divided.

Shareholders. Fourth. The names and places of residence of the shareholders and the number of shares held by each of them.

Object of certificate. Fifth. The fact that the certificate is made to enable such persons to avail themselves of the advantages of this Title.

Acknowledgment of organization certificate. 14. (SEC. 5135.) The organization certificate shall be acknowledged before a judge of some court of record, or notary public; and shall be, together with the acknowledgment thereof, authenticated by the seal of such court, or notary, transmitted to the Comptroller of the Currency, who shall record and carefully preserve the same in his office. .

Corporate powers of associations. 15. (SEC. 5136.) Upon duly making and filing articles of 2 Abb., U. S., association and an organization certificate, the association 416. shall become, as from the date of the execution of its organization certificate, a body corporate, and as such, and in the name designated in the organization certificate, it shall have power—

First. To adopt and use a corporate seal. Seal.

Second. To have succession for the period of twenty years from its organization, unless it is sooner dissolved according to the provisions of its articles of association, or by the act of its shareholders owning two-thirds of its stock, or unless its franchise becomes forfeited by some violation of law. Succession. See act July 12, 1882, page 70.

Third. To make contracts. Contracts.

Fourth. To sue and be sued, complain and defend, in any court of law and [or] equity, as fully as natural persons. Suits.

Fifth. To elect or appoint directors, and by its board of directors to appoint a president, vice-president, cashier, and other officers, define their duties, require bonds of them and fix the penalty thereof, dismiss such officers or any of them at pleasure, and appoint others to fill their places. Appointment of officers.

Sixth. To prescribe, by its board of directors, by-laws not inconsistent with law, regulating the manner in which its stock shall be transferred, its directors elected or appointed, its officers appointed, its property transferred, its general business conducted, and the privileges granted to it by law exercised and enjoyed. By laws.

Seventh. To exercise by its board of directors, or duly authorized officers or agents, subject to law, all such incidental powers as shall be necessary to carry on the business of banking; by discounting and negotiating promissory notes, drafts, bills of exchange, and other evidences of debt; by receiving deposits; by buying and selling exchange, coin, and bullion; by loaning money on personal security; and by obtaining, issuing, and circulating notes according to the provisions of this Title. Incidental powers.

But no association shall transact any business except such as is incidental and necessarily preliminary to its organization, until it has been authorized by the Comptroller of the Currency to commence the business of banking. When may commence business.

16. (SEC. 5137.) A national banking association may purchase, hold, and convey real estate for the following purposes, and for no others: Power to hold real property.

First. Such as shall be necessary for its immediate accommodation in the transaction of its business.

Second. Such as shall be mortgaged to it in good faith by way of security for debts previously contracted.

Third. Such as shall be conveyed to it in satisfaction of debts previously contracted in the course of its dealings.

Fourth. Such as it shall purchase at sales under judgments, decrees, or mortgages held by the association, or shall purchase to secure debts due to it.

Limitation as to mortgages, &c. But no such association shall hold the possession of any real estate under mortgage, or the title and possession of any real estate purchased to secure any debts due to it, for a longer period than five years.

Minimum capital required. 17. (SEC. 5138.) No association shall be organized under this Title with a less capital than one hundred thousand dollars; except that banks with a capital of not less than fifty thousand dollars may, with the approval of the Secretary of the Treasury, be organized in any place the population of which does not exceed six thousand inhabitants. No association shall be organized in a city the population of which exceeds fifty thousand persons with a less capital than two hundred thousand dollars.

Value and transfer of shares of stock. 18. (SEC. 5139.) The capital stock of each association shall be divided into shares of one hundred dollars each, and be deemed personal property, and transferable on the books of the association in such manner as may be prescribed in the by-laws or articles of association. Every person becoming a shareholder by such transfer shall, in proportion to his shares, succeed to all the rights and liabilities of the prior holder of such shares; and no change shall be made in the articles of association by which the rights, remedies, or security of the existing creditors of the association shall be impaired.

Rights and liabilities of persons holding shares by transfer.

Van Allen vs. The Assessors, 3 Wall., 573.

When capital stock must be paid in and certified. 19. (SEC. 5140.) At least fifty per centum of the capital stock of every association shall be paid in before it shall be authorized to commence business; and the remainder of the capital stock of such association shall be paid in installments of at least ten per centum each, on the whole amount of the capital, as frequently as one installment at the end of each succeeding month from the time it shall be authorized by the Comptroller of the Currency to commence business; and the payment of each installment shall be certified to the Comptroller, under oath, by the president or cashier of the association.

Proceedings if shareholder fails to pay installments. 20. (SEC. 5141.) Whenever any shareholder, or his assignee, fails to pay any installment on the stock when the same is required by the preceding section to be paid, the directors of such association may sell the stock of such delinquent shareholder at public auction, having given three weeks' previous notice thereof in a newspaper published and of general circulation in the city or county where the association is located, or if no newspaper is published in said city or county, then in a newspaper published nearest thereto to any person who will pay the highest price therefor, to be not less than the amount then due thereon, with the expenses of advertisement and sale; and the excess, if any, shall be paid to the delinquent shareholder. If no bidder can be found who will pay for such stock the amount due thereon to the association, and the cost of advertisement and sale, the amount previously paid shall be forfeited to the association, and such stock shall be sold as the directors may order, within six months from the time of such forfeiture, and if not sold it shall be canceled and deducted from the capital stock of the association. If any such cancellation and reduction shall reduce the capital of the association below the minimum of capital required by law, the capital stock shall, within thirty days from the date of such cancellation, be increased to the required amount; in default of which a receiver may be appointed, according to the provisions of section fifty-two hundred and thirty-four, to close up the business of the association.

Capital to be restored if reduced below minimum, or receiver appointed.

Section 5142, page 12.

21. (SEC. 5168.) Whenever a certificate is transmitted to the Comptroller of the Currency, as provided in this Title, and the association transmitting the same notifies the Comptroller that at least fifty per centum of its capital stock has been duly paid in, and that such association has complied with all the provisions of this Title required to be complied with before an association shall be authorized to commence the business of banking, the Comptroller shall examine into the condition of such association, ascertain especially the amount of money paid in on account of its capital, the name and place of residence of each of its directors, and the amount of the capital stock of which each is the owner in good faith, and generally whether such association has complied with all the provisions of this Title required to entitle it to engage in the business of banking; and shall cause to be made and attested by the oaths of a majority of the directors, and by the president or cashier of the association, a statement of all the facts necessary to enable the Comptroller to determine whether the association is lawfully entitled to commence the business of banking.

Comptroller to determine if association is entitled to commence business.

Certificate of officers and directors.

12

Certificates of authority to commence business, when to be issued. 22. (SEC. 5169.) If, upon a careful examination of the facts so reported, and of any other facts which may come to the knowledge of the Comptroller, whether by means of a special commission appointed by him for the purpose of inquiring into the condition of such association, or otherwise, it appears that such association is lawfully entitled to commence the business of banking, the Comptroller shall give to such association a certificate, under his hand and official seal, that such association has complied with all the provisions required to be complied with before commencing the business of banking, and that such association is au-

When certificate of authority may be withheld. thorized to commence such business. But the Comptroller may withhold from an association his certificate authorizing the commencement of business, whenever he has reason to suppose that the shareholders have formed the same for any other than the legitimate objects contemplated by this Title.

Publication of certificate. 23. (SEC. 5170.) The association shall cause the certificate issued under the preceding section to be published in some newspaper printed in the city or county where the association is located, for at least sixty days next after the

Section 5171, page 20. issuing thereof; or, if no newspaper is published in such city or county, then in the newspaper published nearest thereto.

Increase of capital stock. 24. (SEC. 5142.) Any association formed under this Title may, by its articles of association, provide for an increase of its capital from time to time, as may be deemed expedient, subject to the limitations of this Title. But the maximum of such increase to be provided in the articles of association shall be determined by the Comptroller of the Currency; and no increase of capital shall be valid until the whole amount of such increase is paid in, and notice thereof has been transmitted to the Comptroller of the Currency, and his certificate obtained specifying the amount of such increase of capital stock, with his approval thereof, and that it has been duly paid in as part of the capital of such association.

Reduction of capital stock. 25. (SEC. 5143.) Any association formed under this Title may, by the vote of shareholders owning two-thirds of its capital stock, reduce its capital to any sum not below the amount required by this Title to authorize the formation of associations; but no such reduction shall be allowable which will reduce the capital of the association below the amount required for its outstanding circulation, nor shall any such reduction be made until the amount of the proposed reduction has been reported to the Comptroller of the Currency and his approval thereof obtained.

26. (SEC. 5144.) In all elections of directors, and in deciding all questions at meetings of shareholders, each shareholder shall be entitled to one vote on each share of stock held by him. Shareholders may vote by proxies duly authorized in writing; but no officer, clerk, teller, or bookkeeper of such association shall act as proxy; and no shareholder whose liability is past due and unpaid shall be allowed to vote.

Rights of shareholders to vote at elections.

Proxies.

27. (SEC. 5145.) The affairs of each association shall be managed by not less than five directors, who shall be elected by the shareholders at a meeting to be held at any time before the association is authorized by the Comptroller of the Currency to commence the business of banking; and afterward at meetings to be held on such day in January of each year as is specified therefor in the articles of association. The directors shall hold office for one year, and until their successors are elected and have qualified.

Number and election of directors.

Term of office.

28. (SEC. 5146.) Every director must, during his whole term of service, be a citizen of the United States, and at least three-fourths of the directors must have resided in the State, Territory, or District in which the association is located, for at least one year immediately preceding their election, and must be residents therein during their continuance in office. Every director must own, in his own right, at least ten shares of the capital stock of the association of which he is a director. Any director who ceases to be the owner of ten shares of the stock, or who becomes in any other manner disqualified, shall thereby vacate his place.

Qualifications of directors.

29. (SEC. 5147.) Each director, when appointed or elected, shall take an oath that he will, so far as the duty devolves on him, diligently and honestly administer the affairs of such association, and will not knowingly violate, or willingly permit to be violated, any of the provisions of this Title, and that he is the owner in good faith, and in his own right, of the number of shares of stock required by this Title, subscribed by him, or standing in his name on the books of the association, and that the same is not hypothecated, or in any way pledged, as security for any loan or debt. Such oath, subscribed by the director making it, and certified by the officer before whom it is taken, shall be immediately trans-

Oath required from directors.

14

mitted to the Comptroller of the Currency, and shall be filed and preserved in his Office.

Vacancies, how filled. 30. (SEC. 5148.) Any vacancy in the board shall be filled by appointment by the remaining directors, and any director so appointed shall hold his place until the next election.

Proceedings where no election is held on the proper day. 31. (SEC. 5149.) If, from any cause, an election of directors is not made at the time appointed, the association shall not for that cause be dissolved, but an election may be held on any subsequent day, thirty days' notice thereof in all cases having been given in a newspaper published in the city, town, or county in which the association is located; and if no newspaper is published in such city, town, or county, such notice shall be published in a newspaper published nearest thereto. If the articles of association do not fix the day on which the election shall be held, or if no election is held on the day fixed, the day for the election shall be designated by the board of directors in their by-laws, or otherwise; or if the directors fail to fix the day, shareholders representing two-thirds of the shares may do so.

The president must be a director. 32. (SEC. 5150.) One of the directors, to be chosen by the board, shall be the president of the board.

Individual liability of shareholders. 33. (SEC. 5151.) The shareholders of every national banking association shall be held individually responsible, equally and ratably, and not one for another, for all contracts, debts, and engagements of such association, to the extent of the amount of their stock therein, at the par value thereof, in addition to the amount invested in such shares; except that **Exception as to individual liability.** shareholders of any banking association now existing under State laws, having not less than five millions of dollars of capital actually paid in, and a surplus of twenty per centum on hand, both to be determined by the Comptroller of the Currency, shall be liable only to the amount invested in their shares; and such surplus of twenty per centum shall be kept undiminished, and be in addition to the surplus provided for in this Title; and if at any time there is a deficiency in such surplus of twenty per centum, such association shall not pay any dividends to its shareholders until the deficiency is made good; and in case of such deficiency, the **Receiver may be appointed for deficiency in surplus.** Comptroller of the Currency may compel the association to close its business and wind up its affairs under the provisions of Chapter four* of this Title.

* Chapter five of this compilation.

34. (SEC. 5152.) Persons holding stock as executors, administrators, guardians, or trustees, shall not be personally subject to any liabilities as stockholders; but the estates and funds in their hands shall be liable in like manner and to the same extent as the testator, intestate, ward, or person interested in such trust-funds would be, if living and competent to act and hold the stock in his own name. *Executors trustees, &c., not personally liable.*

35. (SEC. 5153.) All national banking associations, designated for that purpose by the Secretary of the Treasury, shall be depositaries of public money, except receipts from customs, under such regulations as may be prescribed by the Secretary; and they may also be employed as financial agents of the Government; and they shall perform all such reasonable duties, as depositaries of public moneys and financial agents of the Government, as may be required of them. The Secretary of the Treasury shall require the associations thus designated to give satisfactory security, by the deposit of United States bonds and otherwise, for the safe-keeping and prompt payment of the public money deposited with them, and for the faithful performance of their duties as financial agents of the Government. And every association so designated as receiver or depositary of the public money shall take and receive at par all of the national currency bills, by whatever association issued, which have been paid into the Government for internal revenue, or for loans or stocks. *Duties and liabilities of associations when designated as depositaries of public moneys.*

36. (SEC. 5154.) Any bank incorporated by special law, or any banking institution organized under a general law of any State, may become a national association under this Title by the name prescribed in its organization certificate; and in such case the articles of association and the organization certificate may be executed by a majority of the directors of the bank or banking institution; and the certificate shall declare that the owners of two-thirds of the capital stock have authorized the directors to make such certificate, and to change and convert the bank or banking institution into a national association. A majority of the directors, after executing the articles of association and organization certificate, shall have power to execute all other papers, and to do whatever may be required to make its organization perfect and complete as a national association. The shares of any such bank may continue to be for the same amount each as they were before the conversion, and the directors may continue to be the directors of the asso- *Organization of State banks as national banking associations.* *Mode of procedure.* *Shares and powers of State bank after conversion.*

ciation until others are elected or appointed in accordance with the provisions of this chapter; and any State bank which is a stockholder in any other bank, by authority of State laws, may continue to hold its stock, although either bank, or both, may be organized under and have accepted the provisions of this Title. When the Comptroller of the Currency has given to such association a certificate, under his hand and official seal, that the provisions of this Title have been complied with, and that it is authorized to commence the business of banking, the association shall have the same powers and privileges, and shall be subject to the same duties, responsibilities, and rules, in all respects, as are prescribed for other associations originally organized as national banking associations, and shall be held and regarded as such an association. But no such association shall have a less capital than the amount prescribed for associations organized under this Title.

To have the same rights, liabilities, &c., as other national associations.

Minimum capital.

State banks having branches.
37. (SEC. 5155.) It shall be lawful for any bank or banking association, organized under State laws, and having branches, the capital being joint and assigned to and used by the mother-bank and branches in definite proportions, to become a national banking association in conformity with existing laws, and to retain and keep in operation its branches, or such one or more of them as it may elect to retain; the amount of the circulation redeemable at the mother-bank, and each branch, to be regulated by the amount of capital assigned to and used by each.

Reservation of rights of associations organized under act of 1863.
38. (SEC. 5156.) Nothing in this Title shall affect any appointments made, acts done, or proceedings had or commenced prior to the third day of June, eighteen hundred and sixty-four, in or toward the organization of any national banking association under the act of February twenty-five, eighteen hundred and sixty-three; but all associations which, on the third day of June, eighteen hundred and sixty-four, were organized or commenced to be organized under that act, shall enjoy all the rights and privileges granted, and be subject to all the duties, liabilities, and restrictions imposed by this Title, notwithstanding all the steps prescribed by this Title for the organization of associations were not pursued, if such associations were duly organized under that act.

17

CHAPTER THREE.

OBTAINING AND ISSUING CIRCULATING NOTES.

39. (SEC. 5157.) The provisions of chapters two, three, ^{What associations are governed by chapters 2, 3, and 4 of this Title.*} and four* of this Title, which are expressed without restrictive words, as applying to "national banking associations," or to "associations," apply to all associations organized to carry on the business of banking under any act of Congress.

40. (SEC. 5158.) The term "United States bonds," as used throughout this chapter, shall be construed to mean registered bonds of the United States.

United States bonds defined.

41. (SEC. 5159.) Every association, after having complied with the provisions of this Title, preliminary to the commencement of the banking business, and before it shall be authorized to commence banking business under this Title, shall transfer and deliver to the Treasurer of the United States any United States registered bonds, bearing interest, to an amount not less than thirty thousand dollars and not less than one-third of the capital stock paid in. Such bonds shall be received by the Treasurer upon deposit, and shall be by him safely kept in his office, until they shall be otherwise disposed of, in pursuance of the provisions of this Title.

U. S. bonds to be deposited before commencing business.
See act of June 20, 1874, section 4, page 56.
See act July 12, 1882, section 8, page 74.

42. (SEC. 5160.) The deposits of bonds made by each association shall be increased as its capital may be paid up or increased, so that every association shall at all times have on deposit with the Treasurer registered United States bonds to the amount of at least one-third of its capital stock actually paid in. And any association that may desire to reduce its capital or close up its business and dissolve its organization, may take up its bonds upon returning to the Comptroller its circulating notes in the proportion hereinafter required, or may take up any excess of bonds beyond one-third of its capital stock, and upon which no circulating notes have been delivered.

Bonds to be increased upon increase of capital.
See act July 12, 1882, section 8, page 74.
May be diminished upon reduction of capital.
Ibid.

43. (SEC. 5161.) To facilitate a compliance with the two preceding sections, the Secretary of the Treasury is authorized to receive from any association, and cancel, any United States coupon bonds, and to issue in lieu thereof registered bonds of like amount, bearing a like rate of interest, and having the same time to run.

Exchange of coupon for registered bonds.

---

* Chapters three, four and five of this compilation.

2761—2

18

Transfer of bonds to and by Treasurer. 44. (SEC. 5162.) All transfers of United States bonds, made by any association under the provisions of this Title, shall be made to the Treasurer of the United States in trust for the association, with a memorandum written or printed on each bond, and signed by the cashier, or some other officer of the association making the deposit. A receipt shall be given to the association, by the Comptroller of the Currency, or by a clerk appointed by him for that purpose, stating that the bond is held in trust for the association on whose behalf the transfer is made, and as security for the redemption and payment of any circulating notes that have been or may be delivered to such association. No assignment or transfer of any such bond by the Treasurer shall be deemed valid unless countersigned by the Comptroller of the Currency.

Registry of transfers. 45. (SEC. 5163.) The Comptroller of the Currency shall keep in his office a book in which he shall cause to be entered, immediately upon countersigning it, every transfer or assignment by the Treasurer, of any bonds belonging to a national banking association, presented for his signature. He shall state in such entry the name of the association from whose account the transfer is made, the name of the party to whom it is made, and the par value of the bonds transferred.

Notice of transfer to be given to association. 46. (SEC. 5164.) The Comptroller of the Currency shall, immediately upon countersigning and entering any transfer or assignment by the Treasurer, of any bonds belonging to a national banking association, advise by mail the association from whose accounts the transfer is made, of the kind and numerical designation of the bonds, and the amount thereof so transferred.

Comptroller to have access to bonds, and to books of Treasurer. 47. (SEC. 5165.) The Comptroller of the Currency shall have at all times, during office-hours, access to the books of the Treasurer of the United States for the purpose of ascertaining the correctness of any transfer or assignment of the bonds deposited by an association, presented to the Comptroller to countersign; and the Treasurer shall have the like **Treasurer to have access to books of Comptroller.** access to the book mentioned in section fifty-one hundred and sixty-three, during office-hours, to ascertain the correctness of the entries in the same; and the Comptroller shall also at all times have access to the bonds on deposit with the Treasurer, to ascertain their amount and condition.

19

48. (SEC. 5166.) Every association having bonds deposited in the office of the Treasurer of the United States shall, once or oftener in each fiscal year, examine and compare the bonds pledged by the association with the books of the Comptroller of the Currency and with the accounts of the association, and, if they are found correct, to execute to the Treasurer a certificate setting forth the different kinds and the amounts thereof, and that the same are in the possession and custody of the Treasurer at the date of the certificate. Such examination shall be made at such time or times, during the ordinary business hours, as the Treasurer and the Comptroller, respectively, may select, and may be made by an officer or agent of such association, duly appointed in writing for that purpose; and his certificate before mentioned shall be of like force and validity as if executed by the president or cashier. A duplicate of such certificate, signed by the Treasurer, shall be retained by the association.

Annual examination of bonds by associations.

49. (SEC. 5167.) The bonds transferred to and deposited with the Treasurer of the United States, by any association, for the security of its circulating notes, shall be held exclusively for that purpose, until such notes are redeemed, except as provided in this Title. The Comptroller of the Currency shall give to any such association powers of attorney to receive and appropriate to its own use the interest on the bonds which it has so transferred to the Treasurer; but such powers shall become inoperative whenever such association fails to redeem its circulating notes. Whenever the market or cash value of any bonds thus deposited with the Treasurer is reduced below the amount of the circulation issued for the same, the Comptroller may demand and receive the amount of such depreciation in other United States bonds at cash value, or in money, from the association, to be deposited with the Treasurer as long as such depreciation continues. And the Comptroller, upon the terms prescribed by the Secretary of the Treasury, may permit an exchange to be made of any of the bonds deposited with the Treasurer by any association for other bonds of the United States authorized to be received as security for circulating notes, if he is of opinion that such an exchange can be made without prejudice to the United States; and he may direct the return of any bonds to the association which transferred the same, in sums of not less than one thousand dollars, upon

Bonds to be held to secure circulation.

Interest on bonds, how collected.

If bonds depreciate, deposit to be increased.

Exchange of bonds.

Return of bonds on surrender of circulation.

20

the surrender to him and the cancellation of a proportion-

ate amount of such circulating notes: *Provided,* That the remaining bonds which shall have been transferred by the association offering to surrender circulating notes are equal to the amount required for the circulating notes not surrendered by such association, and that the amount of bonds in the hands of the Treasurer is not diminished below the amount required to be kept on deposit with him, and that there has been no failure by the association to redeem its circulating notes, nor any other violation by it of the provisions of this Title, and that the market or cash value of the remaining bonds is not below the amount required for the circulation issued for the same.

Limitation on withdrawal of bonds.

See act of June 20, 1874, section 4, page 56.

Sections 5168, 5169, and 5170, pages 11 and 12.

Delivery of circulating notes to associations.

50. (SEC. 5171.) Upon a deposit of bonds as prescribed by sections fifty-one hundred and fifty-nine and fifty-one hundred and sixty, the association making the same shall be entitled to receive from the Comptroller of the Currency circulating notes of different denominations, in blank, registered and countersigned as hereinafter provided, equal in amount to ninety per centum of the current market-value of the United States bonds so transferred and delivered, but not exceeding ninety per centum of the amount of the bonds at the par value thereof, if bearing interest at a rate not less than five per centum per annum: *Provided,* That the amount of circulating notes to be furnished to each association shall be in proportion to its paid-up capital, as follows, and no more:

Modified by act July 12, 1882, section 10, page 75.

Ratio to capital of circulating notes issued.

First. To each association whose capital does not exceed five hundred thousand dollars, ninety per centum of such capital.

Repealed by section 10, act July 12, 1882, page 75.

Second. To each association whose capital exceeds five hundred thousand dollars, but does not exceed one million of dollars, eighty per centum of such capital.

Third. To each association whose capital exceeds one million of dollars, but does not exceed three million [s] of dollars, seventy-five per centum of such capital.

Fourth. To each association whose capital exceeds three millions of dollars, sixty per centum of such capital.

Form, denominations, and printing of circulating notes.

51. (SEC. 5172.) In order to furnish suitable notes for circulation, the Comptroller of the Currency shall, under the direction of the Secretary of the Treasury, cause plates and dies to be engraved, in the best manner to guard against

counterfeiting and fraudulent alterations, and shall have
printed therefrom, and numbered, such quantity of circulating notes, in blank, of the denominations of one dollar, two
dollars, three dollars, five dollars, ten dollars, twenty dollars,
fifty dollars, one hundred dollars, five hundred dollars, and
one thousand dollars, as may be required to supply the associations entitled to receive the same. Such notes shall
express upon their face that they are secured by United
States bonds, deposited with the Treasurer of the United
States, by the written or engraved signatures of the Treasurer and Register, and by the imprint of the seal of the
Treasury; and shall also express upon their face the promise of the association receiving the same to pay on demand,
attested by the signatures of the president or vice-president and cashier; and shall bear such devices and such other
statements, and shall be in such form, as the Secretary of
the Treasury shall, by regulation, direct.

52. (SEC. 5173.) The plates and special dies to be pro- *Control of plates and dies, and expenses of Bureau.*
cured by the Comptroller of the Currency for the printing
of such circulating notes shall remain under his control and
direction, and the expenses necessarily incurred in executing *See section 3, act June 20, 1874, page 55, and sec-*
the laws respecting the procuring of such notes, and all *tion 8, act July*
other expenses of the Bureau of the Currency, shall be paid *12, 1882, page 74.*
out of the proceeds of the taxes or duties assessed and collected on the circulation of national banking associations
under this Title.

53. (SEC. 5174.) The Comptroller of the Currency shall *Annual exami- nation of plates, dies, &c.*
cause to be examined, each year, the plates, dies, but-pieces,
[bed-pieces,] and other material from which the national-
bank circulation is printed, in whole or in part, and file in
his Office annually a correct list of the same. Such mate- *Certain print- ing material to be destroyed.*
rial as shall have been used in the printing of the notes of
associations which are in liquidation, or have closed business, shall be destroyed under such regulations as shall be
prescribed by the Comptroller of the Currency and approved
by the Secretary of the Treasury. The expenses of any such
examination or destruction shall be paid out of any appropriation made by Congress for the special examination of
national banks and bank-note plates.

54. (SEC. 5175.) Not more than one-sixth part of the notes *Issue of notes under five dol- lars, limited.*
furnished to any association shall be of a less denomination
than five dollars. After specie payments are resumed no

association shall be furnished with notes of a less denomination than five dollars.

Circulation of certain banks limited to $500,000.
Repealed by act July 12, 1882, section 10, page 75.

55. (SEC. 5176.) No banking association organized subsequent to the twelfth day of July, eighteen hundred and seventy, shall have a circulation in excess of five hundred thousand dollars.

Aggregate amount of circulating notes.
Superseded by act Jan. 14, 1875, sec. 3, page 60.

56. (SEC. 5177.) The aggregate amount of circulating notes issued under the act of February twenty-five, eighteen hundred and sixty-three, and under the act of June three, eighteen hundred and sixty-four, and under section one of the act of July twelve, eighteen hundred and seventy, and under this Title, shall not exceed three hundred and fifty-four millions of dollars.

Apportionment of circulating notes.
Superseded by act Jan. 14, 1875, sec. 3, page 60.

57. (SEC. 5178.) One hundred and fifty millions of dollars of the entire amount of circulating notes authorized to be issued shall be apportioned to associations in the States, in the Territories, and in the District of Columbia, according to representative population. One hundred and fifty millions shall be apportioned by the Secretary of the Treasury among associations formed in the several States, in the Territories, and in the District of Columbia, having due regard to the existing banking capital, resources, and business of such States, Territories, and District. The remaining fifty-four millions shall be apportioned among associations in States and Territories having, under the apportionments above prescribed, less than their full proportion of the aggregate amount of notes authorized, which made due application for circulating notes prior to the twelfth day of July, eighteen hundred and seventy-one. Any remainder of such fifty-four millions shall be issued to banking associations applying for circulating notes in other States or Territories having less than their proportion.

Equalizing the distribution of circulating notes.
Superseded by act Jan. 14, 1875, sec. 3, page 60.

58. (SEC. 5179.) In order to secure a more equitable distribution of the national banking currency, there may be issued circulating notes to banking associations organized in States and Territories having less than their proportion, and the amount of circulation herein authorized shall, under the direction of the Secretary of the Treasury, as it may be required for this purpose, be withdrawn, as herein provided, from banking associations organized in States having more than their proportion, but the amount so withdrawn shall not exceed twenty-five million dollars: *Provided,* That no cir-

See act of June 20, 1874, section 7, page 57.

culation shall be withdrawn under the provisions of this
section until after the fifty-four millions granted in the first
section of the act of July twelfth, eighteen hundred and
seventy, shall have been taken up.

59. (SEC. 5180.) The Comptroller of the Currency shall,
under the direction of the Secretary of the Treasury, make
a statement showing the amount of circulation in each State
and Territory, and the amount necessary to be withdrawn
from each association, and shall forthwith make a requisition
for such amount upon such associations, commencing with
those having a circulation exceeding one million of dollars,
in States having an excess of circulation, and withdrawing
their circulation in excess of one million of dollars, and then
proceeding proportionately with other associations having a
circulation exceeding three hundred thousand dollars, in
States having the largest excess of circulation, and reduc-
ing the circulation of such associations in States having the
greatest proportion in excess, leaving undisturbed the associations in States having a smaller proportion, until those
in greater excess have been reduced to the same grade,
and continuing thus to make such reductions until the full
amount of twenty-five millions has been withdrawn; and
the circulation so withdrawn shall be distributed among the
States and Territories having less than their proportion, so
as to equalize the same. Upon failure of any association
to return the amount of circulating notes so required, within
one year, the Comptroller shall sell at public auction, having given twenty days' notice thereof in one daily newspaper printed in Washington and one in New York City, an
amount of the bonds deposited by that association as security for its circulation, equal to the circulation required
to be withdrawn from the association and not returned in
compliance with such requisition; and he shall, with the
proceeds, redeem so many of the notes of such association,
as they come into the Treasury, as will equal the amount
required and not returned; and shall pay the balance, if
any, to the association.

60. (SEC. 5181.) Any association located in any State
having more than its proportion of circulation may be removed to any State having less than its proportion of circulation, under such rules and regulations as the Comptroller of the Currency, with the approval of the Secretary

Marginal notes: Method of procedure in with-drawing excess of circulation. See act of Jan. 14, 1875 section 3, page 60. — Sale of bonds upon failure of association to return notes. — Removal of associations from State having an excess of circulation to one having a deficiency. See act of Jan. 14, 1875, section 2, page 60.

of the Treasury, shall prescribe: *Provided*, That the amount of the issue of said banks shall not be deducted from the issue of fifty-four millions mentioned in section five thousand one hundred and seventy-eight.

Circulating notes, when may be issued by associations.

61. (SEC. 5182.) After any association receiving circulating notes under this Title has caused its promise to pay such notes on demand to be signed by the president or vice-president and cashier thereof, in such manner as to make them obligatory promissory notes, payable on demand, at its place of business, such association may issue and circulate the same as money.

For what demands shall be received.

And the same shall be received at par in all parts of the United States in payment of taxes, excises, public lands, and all other dues to the United States, except duties on exports; and also for all salaries and other debts and demands owing by the United States to individuals, corporations, and associations within the United States, except interest on the public debt, and in redemption of the national currency.

Issue of other notes prohibited. See act of Feb. 18, 1875, correcting Rev. Stats., page 63.

62. (SEC. 5183.) No national banking association shall issue post-notes or any other notes to circulate as money than such as are authorized by the provisions of this Title. Merchants' Bank *vs.* State Bank, 10 Wall. 604.

Destroying and replacing worn-out and mutilated notes.

63. (SEC. 5184.) It shall be the duty of the Comptroller of the Currency to receive worn-out or mutilated circulating notes issued by any banking association, and also, on due proof of the destruction of any such circulating notes, to deliver in place thereof to the association other blank circulating notes to an equal amount. Such worn-out or mutilated notes, after a memorandum has been entered in the proper books, in accordance with such regulations as may be established by the Comptroller, as well as all circulating notes which shall have been paid or surrendered to be can-

Modified by act of June 23, 1874, page 59.

celed, shall be burned to ashes in presence of four persons, one to be appointed by the Secretary of the Treasury, one by the Comptroller of the Currency, one by the Treasurer of the United States, and one by the association, under such regulations as the Secretary of the Treasury may prescribe. A certificate of such burning, signed by the parties so appointed, shall be made in the books of the Comptroller, and a duplicate thereof forwarded to the association whose notes are thus canceled.

Organization of associations for issuing gold notes.

64. (SEC. 5185.) Associations may be organized in the manner prescribed by this Title for the purpose of issuing

notes payable in gold; and upon the deposit of any United States bonds bearing interest payable in gold with the Treasurer of the United States, in the manner prescribed for other associations, it shall be lawful for the Comptroller of the Currency to issue to the association making the deposit circulating notes of different denominations, but none of them of less than five dollars, and not exceeding in amount eighty per centum of the par value of the bonds deposited, which shall express the promise of the association to pay them, upon presentation at the office at which they are issued, in gold coin of the United States, and shall be so redeemable. But no such association shall have a circulation of more than one million of dollars. *See act Feb. 1 1880, page 69.*

Denominations of circulating notes, and ratio of to bonds deposited.

Maximum circulation. See act of Jan. 19, 1875, page 61.

65. (SEC. 5186.) Every association organized under the preceding section shall at all times keep on hand not less than twenty-five per centum of its outstanding circulation, in gold or silver coin of the United States; and shall receive at par in the payment of debts the gold-notes of every other such association which at the time of such payment is redeeming its circulating notes in gold coin of the United States, and shall be subject to all the provisions of this Title: *Provided,* That, in applying the same to associations organized for issuing gold-notes, the terms "lawful money" and "lawful money of the United States" shall be construed to mean gold or silver coin of the United States; and the circulation of such association shall not be within the limitation of circulation mentioned in this Title. *Reserve required on circulation of gold-banks.*

Gold-notes to be received at par by all gold-banks.

"Lawful money," how construed.

Section 5187, page 46.

66. (SEC. 5188.) It shall not be lawful to design, engrave, print, or in any manner make or execute, or to utter, issue, distribute, circulate, or use, any business or professional card, notice, placard, circular, hand-bill, or advertisement, in the likeness or similitude of any circulating note or other obligation or security of any banking association organized or acting under the laws of the United States which has been or may be issued under this Title, or any act of Congress, or to write, print, or otherwise impress upon any such note, obligation, or security any business or professional card, notice or advertisement, or any notice or advertisement of any matter or thing whatever. Every person who violates this section shall be liable to a penalty of one hundred dollars, recoverable one-half to the use of the informer. *Penalty for imitating national-bank notes, &c.*

Penalty for mutilating national-bank notes, &c.

67. (SEC. 5189.) Every person who mutilates, cuts, defaces, disfigures, or perforates with holes, or unites or cements together, or does any other thing to any bank-bill, draft, note, or other evidence of debt, issued by any national banking association, or who causes or procures the same to be done, with intent to render such bank-bill, draft, note, or other evidence of debt unfit to be re-issued by said association, shall be liable to a penalty of fifty dollars, recoverable by the association.

CHAPTER FOUR.

REGULATION OF THE BANKING BUSINESS.

Place of business.
Merchants' Bank vs. State Bank, 10 Wall., 604.

68. (SEC. 5190.) The usual business of each national banking association shall be transacted at an office or banking-house located in the place specified in its organization certificate.

Requirements as to lawful money reserve.
See act of June 20, 1874, section 2, page 55.

No loans or dividends to be made while reserve is below limit.

See act July 12, 1882, section 12, page 76.

69. (SEC. 5191.) Every national banking association in either of the following cities: Albany, Baltimore, Boston, Cincinnati, Chicago, Cleveland, Detroit, Louisville, Milwaukee, New Orleans, New York, Philadelphia, Pittsburgh, Saint Louis, San Francisco, and Washington, shall at all times have on hand, in lawful money of the United States, an amount equal to at least twenty-five per centum of the aggregate amount of its notes in circulation and its deposits; and every other association shall at all times have on hand, in lawful money of the United States, an amount equal to at least fifteen per centum of the aggregate amount of its notes in circulation, and of its deposits. Whenever the lawful money of any association in any of the cities named shall be below the amount of twenty-five per centum of its circulation and deposits, and whenever the lawful money of any other association shall be below fifteen per centum of its circulation and deposits, such association shall not increase its liabilities by making any new loans or discounts otherwise than by discounting or purchasing bills of exchange payable at sight, nor make any dividend of its profits until the required proportion, between the aggregate amount of its outstanding notes of circulation and deposits and its lawful money of the United States, has been restored. And the Comptroller of the Currency may notify any association, whose lawful-money reserve shall be below the amount above

required to be kept on hand, to make good such reserve; and if such association shall fail for thirty days thereafter so to make good its reserve of lawful money, the Comptroller may, with the concurrence of the Secretary of the Treasury, appoint a receiver to wind up the business of the association, as provided in section fifty-two hundred and thirty-four. *Receiver may be appointed for failure to make good the reserve.*

70. (SEC. 5192.) Three-fifths of the reserve of fifteen per centum required by the preceding section to be kept, may consist of balances due to an association, available for the redemption of its circulating notes, from associations approved by the Comptroller of the Currency, organized under the act of June three, eighteen hundred and sixty-four, or under this Title, and doing business in the cities of Albany, Baltimore, Boston, Charleston, Chicago, Cincinnati, Cleveland, Detroit, Louisville, Milwaukee, New Orleans, New York, Philadelphia, Pittsburgh, Richmond, Saint Louis, San Francisco, and Washington. Clearing-house certificates, representing specie or lawful money specially deposited for the purpose, of any clearing-house association, shall also be deemed to be lawful money in the possession of any association belonging to such clearing-house, holding and owning such certificate, within the preceding section. *Redemption cities, and proportion of reserve which may be kept therein. See act of June 20, 1874, section 3, page 55. Clearing-house certificates deemed lawful money.*

71. (SEC. 5193.) The Secretary of the Treasury may receive United States notes on deposit, without interest, from any national banking associations, in sums of not less than ten thousand dollars, and issue certificates therefor in such form as he may prescribe, in denominations of not less than five thousand dollars, and payable on demand in United States notes at the place where the deposits were made. The notes so deposited shall not be counted as part of the lawful-money reserve of the association; but the certificates issued therefor may be counted as part of its lawful-money reserve, and may be accepted in the settlement of clearing-house balances at the places where the deposits therefor were made. *U. S. certificates of deposit may be issued, and may count as reserve.*

72. (SEC. 5194.) The power conferred on the Secretary of the Treasury, by the preceding section, shall not be exercised so as to create any expansion or contraction of the currency. And United States notes for which certificates are issued under that section, or other United States notes of like amount, shall be held as special deposits in the Treasury, and used only for redemption of such certificates. *Limitation upon the issue of certificates of deposit.*

73. (SEC. 5195.) Each association organized in any of the cities named in section fifty-one hundred and ninety-one shall select, subject to the approval of the Comptroller of the Currency, an association in the city of New York, at which it will redeem its circulating notes at par; and may keep one-half of its lawful-money reserve in cash deposits in the city of New York. But the foregoing provision shall not apply to associations organized and located in the city of San Francisco for the purpose of issuing notes payable in gold. Each association not organized within the cities named, shall select, subject to the approval of the Comptroller, an association in either of the cities named, at which it will redeem its circulating notes at par. The Comptroller shall give public notice of the names of the associations selected, at which redemptions are to be made by the respective associations, and of any change that may be made of the association at which the notes of any association are redeemed. Whenever any association fails either to make the selection or to redeem its notes as aforesaid, the Comptroller of the Currency may, upon receiving satisfactory evidence thereof, appoint a receiver in the manner provided for in section fifty-two hundred and thirty-four, to wind up its affairs. But this section shall not relieve any association from its liability to redeem its circulating notes at its own counter, at par, in lawful money on demand.

Agents for redemption of circulating notes to be designated. See act of June 20, 1874, section 3, page 56.

Receiver may be appointed for failure to redeem notes.

74. (SEC. 5196.) Every national banking association formed or existing under this Title, shall take and receive at par, for any debt or liability to it, any and all notes or bills issued by any lawfully organized national banking association. But this provision shall not apply to any association organized for the purpose of issuing notes payable in gold.

National banks to receive notes of all other national banks.

75. (SEC. 5197.) Any association may take, receive, reserve, and charge on any loan or discount made, or upon any note, bill of exchange, or other evidences of debt, interest at the rate allowed by the laws of the State, Territory, or district where the bank is located, and no more, except that where by the laws of any State a different rate is limited for banks of issue organized under State laws, the rate so limited shall be allowed for associations organized or existing in any such State under this Title. When no rate is fixed by the laws of the State, or Territory, or district, the bank may take, receive, reserve, or charge a rate not exceed-

Limitations upon rate of interest which may be taken. Tiffany vs. National Bank of Missouri, 18 Wall., 409.

ing seven per centum, and such interest may be taken in
advance, reckoning the days from which the note, bill, or
other evidence of debt has to run. And the purchase, dis- The purchase
count, or sale of a bona-fide bill of exchange, payable at bills of exchange,
another place than the place of such purchase, discount, or not usury.
sale, at not more than the current rate of exchange for
sight-drafts in addition to the interest, shall not be considered as taking or receiving a greater rate of interest.

76. (SEC. 5198.)* The taking, receiving, reserving, or charg- Penalty for
ing a rate of interest greater than is allowed by the pre- interest.
ceding section, when knowingly done, shall be deemed a
forfeiture of the entire interest which the note, bill, or other
evidence of debt carries with it, or which has been agreed
to be paid thereon. In case the greater rate of interest has
been paid, the person by whom it has been paid, or his legal
representatives, may recover back, in an action in the nature of an action of debt, twice the amount of the interest
thus paid from the association taking or receiving the same;
provided such action is commenced within two years from
the time the usurious transaction occurred.

77. (SEC. 5199.) The directors of any association may, Dividends and
semi-annually, declare a dividend of so much of the net surplus fund.
profits of the association as they shall judge expedient; but
each association shall, before the declaration of a dividend,
carry one-tenth part of its net profits of the preceding half-
year to its surplus fund until the same shall amount to
twenty per centum of its capital stock.

78. (SEC. 5200.) The total liabilities to any association, of Limit of liabili-
any person, or of any company, corporation, or firm for tion of any per-
money borrowed, including, in the liabilities of a company poration.
or firm, the liabilities of the several members thereof, shall
at no time exceed one-tenth part of the amount of the cap-
ital stock of such association actually paid in. But the dis- The discount of
count of bills of exchange drawn in good faith against &c., not a loan.
actually existing values, and the discount of commercial or
business paper actually owned by the person negotiating
the same, shall not be considered as money borrowed.

79. (SEC. 5201.) No association shall make any loan or Associations
discount on the security of the shares of its own capital or purchase, their
stock, nor be the purchaser or holder of any such shares, own stock.
unless such security or purchase shall be necessary to pre- Bank vs. Lan-
Ballard vs. Bank,
18 Wall., 589.

* For part of section 5198, see page 51, under head of Suits and Jurisdiction.

vent loss upon a debt previously contracted in good faith; and stock so purchased or acquired shall, within six months from the time of its purchase, be sold or disposed of at pub-

Receiver may be appointed for failure to sell stock. lic or private sale; or, in default thereof, a receiver may be appointed to close up the business of the association, according to section fifty-two hundred and thirty-four.

Limit of indebtedness of association. 80. (SEC. 5202.) No association shall at any time be indebted, or in any way liable, to an amount exceeding the amount of its capital stock at such time actually paid in and remaining undiminished by losses or otherwise, except on account of demands of the nature following:

Exceptions. First. Notes of circulation.

Second. Moneys deposited with or collected by the association.

Third. Bills of exchange or drafts drawn against money actually on deposit to the credit of the association, or due thereto.

Fourth. Liabilities to the stockholders of the association for dividends and reserve profits.

Circulating notes not to be hypothecated, nor used to increase capital. 81. (SEC. 5203.) No association shall, either directly or indirectly, pledge or hypothecate any of its notes of circulation, for the purpose of procuring money to be paid in on its capital stock, or to be used in its banking operations, or otherwise; nor shall any association use its circulating notes, or any part thereof, in any manner or form, to create or increase its capital stock.

Withdrawal of capital prohibited. 82. (SEC. 5204.) No association, or any member thereof, shall, during the time it shall continue its banking operations, withdraw, or permit to be withdrawn, either in the form of dividends or otherwise, any portion of its capital. If losses have at any time been sustained by any such association, equal to or exceeding its undivided profits then on hand, no dividend shall be made; and no dividend shall ever be made by any association, while it continues its banking operations, to an amount greater than its net profits then on hand, deducting therefrom its losses and bad debts.

Dividend not to exceed net profits.

Bad debts defined. All debts due to any associations, on which interest is past due and unpaid for a period of six months, unless the same are well secured, and in process of collection, shall be considered bad debts within the meaning of this section. But nothing in this section shall prevent the reduction of the capital stock of the association under section fifty-one hundred and forty-three.

83. (SEC. 5205.) Every association which shall have failed Enforcing payment of deficiency in capital stock. to pay up its capital stock, as required by law, and every association whose capital stock shall have become impaired by losses or otherwise, shall, within three months after receiving notice thereof from the Comptroller of the Currency, pay the deficiency in the capital stock, by assessment upon the shareholders pro rata for the amount of capital stock held by each; and the Treasurer of the United States shall withhold the interest upon all bonds held by him in trust for any such association, upon notification from the Comptroller of the Currency, until otherwise notified by him. If any such association shall fail to pay up its capital Receiver may be appointed for failure to pay up capital. stock, and shall refuse to go into liquidation, as provided by law, for three months after receiving notice from the Comptroller, a receiver may be appointed to close up the business See act June 30, 1876, section 4, page 68. of the association, according to the provisions of section fifty-two hundred and thirty-four.

84. (SEC. 5206.) No association shall at any time pay out Association not to pay out uncurrent notes. on loans or discounts, or in purchasing drafts or bills of exchange, or in payment of deposits, or in any other mode pay or put in circulation, the notes of any bank or banking association which are not, at any such time, receivable, at par, on deposit, and in payment of debts by the association so paying out or circulating such notes; nor shall any association knowingly pay out or put in circulation any notes is ued by any bank or banking association which at the time of such paying out or putting in circulation is not re- Section 5207, page 46. deeming its circulating notes in lawful money of the United States.

85. (SEC. 5208.) It shall be unlawful for any officer, clerk, Penalty for falsely certifying checks. or agent of any national banking association to certify any check drawn upon the association unless the person or company drawing the check has on deposit with the association, at the time such check is certified, an amount of money equal to the amount specified in such check. Any check so certified by duly authorized officers shall be a good and valid obligation against the association; but the act of any Receiver may be appointed for false certification. officer, clerk, or agent of any association, in violation of this section, shall subject such bank to the liabilities and proceedings on the part of the Comptroller as provided for in Section 5209, page 46. section fifty-two hundred and thirty-four.

List of shareholders to be kept, subject to inspection.

86. (SEC. 5210.) The president and cashier of every national banking association shall cause to be kept at all times a full and correct list of the names and residences of all the shareholders in the association, and the number of shares held by each, in the office where its business is transacted. Such list shall be subject to the inspection of all the shareholders and creditors of the association, and the officers authorized to assess taxes under State authority, during business-hours of each day in which business may be legally transacted. A copy of such list, on the first Monday of July of each year, verified by the oath of such president or cashier, shall be transmitted to the Comptroller of the Currency.

List to be sent to Comptroller, annually.

Provisions relative to reports of associations to Comptroller.
See act of Feb. 26, 1881, page 70.

87. (SEC. 5211.) Every association shall make to the Comptroller of the Currency not less than five reports during each year, according to the form which may be prescribed by him, verified by the oath or affirmation of the president or cashier of such association, and attested by the signature of at least three of the directors. Each such report shall exhibit, in detail and under appropriate heads, the resources and liabilities of the associations at the close of business on any past day by him specified; and shall be transmitted to the Comptroller within five days after the receipt of a request or requisition therefor from him, and in the same form in which it is made to the Comptroller shall be published in a newspaper published in the place where such association is established, or if there is no newspaper in the place, then in one published nearest thereto in the same county, at the expense of the association; and such proof of publication shall be furnished as may be required by the Comptroller. The Comptroller shall also have power to call for special reports from any particular association whenever in his judgment the same are necessary in order to a full and complete knowledge of its condition.

Reports of dividends and earnings.

88. (SEC. 5212.) In addition to the reports required by the preceding section, each association shall report to the Comptroller of the Currency, within ten days after declaring any dividend, the amount of such dividend, and the amount of net earnings in excess of such dividend. Such reports shall be attested by the oath of the president or cashier of the association.

89. (SEC. 5213.) Every association which fails to make **Penalty for failure to make reports to Comptroller.** and transmit any report required under either of the two preceding sections shall be subject to a penalty of one hundred dollars for each day after the periods, respectively, therein mentioned, that it delays to make and transmit its report. Whenever any association delays or refuses to pay the penalty herein imposed, after it has been assessed by the Comptroller of the Currency, the amount thereof may be retained by the Treasurer of the United States, upon the order of the Comptroller of the Currency, out of the interest, as it may become due to the association, on the bonds deposited with him to secure circulation. All sums of money collected for penalties under this section shall be paid into the Treasury of the United States.

90. (SEC. 5214.) In lieu of all existing taxes, every association shall pay to the Treasurer of the United States, in **Duty on circulation, deposits, and capital stock.** the months of January and July, a duty of one-half of one per centum each half-year upon the average amount of its notes in circulation, and a duty of one quarter of one per centum each half-year upon the average amount of its deposits, and a duty of one-quarter of one per centum each half-year on the average amount of its capital stock, beyond the amount invested in United States bonds.

91. (SEC. 5215.) In order to enable the Treasurer to assess the duties imposed by the preceding section, each association shall, within ten days from the first days of January **Semi-annual return of circulation, deposits, and capital stock.** and July of each year, make a return, under the oath of its president or cashier, to the Treasurer of the United States, in such form as the Treasurer may prescribe, of the average amount of its notes in circulation, and of the average amount of its deposits, and of the average amount of its capital stock, beyond the amount invested in United States bonds, for the six months next preceding the most recent first day of January or July. Every association which fails so to make such return shall be liable to a penalty of two hundred **Penalty for failure to make return.** dollars, to be collected either out of the interest as it may become due such association on the bonds deposited with the Treasurer, or, at his option, in the manner in which penalties are to be collected of other corporations under the laws of the United States.

92. (SEC. 5216.) Whenever any association fails to make **Method of assessment if return is not made.** the half yearly return required by the preceding section,

2761——3

the duties to be paid by such association shall be assessed
upon the amount of notes delivered to such association
by the Comptroller of the Currency, and upon the highest
amount of its deposits and capital stock, to be ascertained
in such manner as the Treasurer may deem best.

How tax may be collected if association fails to pay. 93. (SEC. 5217.) Whenever an association fails to pay the duties imposed by the three preceding sections, the sums due may be collected in the manner provided for the collection of United States taxes from other corporations; or the Treasurer may reserve the amount out of the interest, as it may become due, on the bonds deposited with him by such defaulting association.

Refunding excess of duties paid. 94. (SEC. 5218.) In all cases where an association has paid or may pay in excess of what may be or has been found due from it, on account of the duty required to be paid to the Treasurer of the United States, the association may state an account therefor, which, on being certified by the Treasurer of the United States, and found correct by the First Comptroller of the Treasury, shall be refunded in the ordinary manner by warrant on the Treasury.

Provisions relative to State taxation of associations.

Bank of Commerce vs. New York City, 2 Bl., 620; Van Allen vs. The Assessors, 3 Wall., 573; People vs. The Commissioners, 4 Wall., 244; Bradley vs. The People, 4 Wall., 459; National Bank vs. The Commonwealth, 9 Wall., 353; Lionberger vs Rouse, 9 Wall., 468. 95. (SEC. 5219.) Nothing herein shall prevent all the shares in any association from being included in the valuation of the personal property of the owner or holder of such shares, in assessing taxes imposed by authority of the State within which the association is located; but the legislature of each State may determine and direct the manner and place of taxing all the shares of national banking associations located within the State, subject only to the two restrictions, that the taxation shall not be at a greater rate than is assessed upon other moneyed capital in the hands of individual citizens of such State, and that the shares of any national banking association owned by non-residents of any State shall be taxed in the city or town where the bank is located, and not elsewhere. Nothing herein shall be construed to exempt the real property of associations from either State, county, or municipal taxes, to the same extent, according to its value, as other real property is taxed.

Sections 5220 to 5237, pages 36 to 41.

Appointment, powers, and duties of bank examiners. 96. (SEC. 5240.) The Comptroller of the Currency, with the approval of the Secretary of the Treasury, shall, as often as shall be deemed necessary or proper, appoint a suitable person or persons to make an examination of the affairs of every banking association, who shall have power to make a thorough examination into all the affairs of the association, and, in doing so, to examine any of the officers and agents thereof on oath; and shall make a full and detailed report of the condition of the association to the Comptroller. All persons appointed to be examiners of national banks not located in the redemption-cities specified in section five thousand one hundred and ninety-two of the Revised Statutes of the United States, or in any one of the States of Oregon, California, and Nevada, or in the Territories, shall receive compensation for such examination as follows: For examining national banks having a capital less than one hundred thousand dollars, twenty dollars; those having a capital of one hundred thousand dollars and less than three hundred thousand dollars, twenty-five dollars; those having a capital of three hundred thousand dollars and less than four hundred thousand dollars, thirty-five dollars; those having a capital of four hundred thousand dollars and less than five hundred thousand dollars, forty dollars; those having a capital of five hundred thousand dollars and less than six hundred thousand dollars, fifty dollars; those having a capital of six hundred thousand dollars and over, seventy-five dollars; which amounts shall be assessed by the Comptroller of the Currency upon, and paid by, the respective association so examined, and shall be in lieu of the compensation and mileage heretofore allowed for making said examinations; and persons appointed to make examinations of national banks in the cities named in section five thousand one hundred and ninety-two of the Revised Statutes of the United States, or in any one of the States of Oregon, California, and Nevada, or in the Territories, shall receive such compensation as may be fixed by the Secretary of the Treasury upon the recommendation of the Comptroller of the Currency; and the same shall be assessed and paid in the manner hereinbefore provided. But no person shall be appointed to examine the affairs of any banking association of which he is a director or other officer.

Compensation of examiners. See act of Feb. 19, 1875, amending Rev. Stats., page 64. See act July 12, 1882, section 3, page 71.

Not to examine banks of which they are officers.

97. (SEC. 5241.) No association shall be subject to any visitorial powers other than such as are authorized by this Title, or are vested in the courts of justice.

Limitation of visitorial powers. Section 5242, page 41.

98. (SEC. 5243.) All banks not organized and transacting business under the national-currency laws, or under this Title, and all persons or corporations doing the business of

Use of the word "national" in title, prohibited to other than national banks.

bankers, brokers, or savings institutions, except savings-banks authorized by Congress to use the word "national" as a part of their corporate name, are prohibited from using the word "national" as a portion of the name or title of such bank, corporation, firm, or partnership; and any violation of this prohibition committed after the third day of September, eighteen hundred and seventy-three, shall subject the party chargeable therewith to a penalty of fifty dollars for each day during which it is committed or repeated.

CHAPTER FIVE.

DISSOLUTION AND RECEIVERSHIP.

Voluntary liquidation. 99. (SEC. 5220.) Any association may go into liquidation and be closed by the vote of its shareholders owning two-thirds of its stock.

Notice of intention to go into liquidation. 100. (SEC. 5221.) Whenever a vote is taken to go into liquidation it shall be the duty of the board of directors to cause notice of this fact to be certified, under the seal of the association, by its president or cashier, to the Comptroller of the Currency, and the publication thereof to be made for a period of two months in a newspaper published in the city of New York, and also in a newspaper published in the city or town in which the association is located, or if no newspaper is there published, then in the newspaper published nearest thereto, that the association is closing up its affairs, and notifying the holders of its notes and other creditors to present the notes and other claims against the association for payment.

Deposit of lawful money to redeem circulation. 101. (SEC. 5222.) Within six months from the date of the vote to go into liquidation, the association shall deposit with the Treasurer of the United States lawful money of the United States sufficient to redeem all its outstanding circulation. The Treasurer shall execute duplicate receipts for money thus deposited, and deliver one to the association and the other to the Comptroller of the Currency, stating the amount received by him, and the purpose for which it has been received; and the money shall be paid into the Treasury of the United States, and placed to the credit of such association upon redemption account.

Consolidating banks need not deposit lawful money. 102. (SEC. 5223.) An association which is in good faith winding up its business for the purpose of consolidating with another association shall not be required to deposit lawful money for its outstanding circulation; but its assets and liabilities shall be reported by the association with which it is in process of consolidation.

103. (SEC. 5224.) Whenever a sufficient deposit of lawful money to redeem the outstanding circulation of an association proposing to close its business has been made, the bonds deposited by the association to secure payment of its notes shall be re-assigned to it, in the manner prescribed by section fifty-one hundred and sixty-two. And thereafter the association and its shareholders shall stand discharged from all liabilities upon the circulating notes, and those notes shall be redeemed at the Treasury of the United States. And if any such bank shall fail to make the deposit and take up its bonds for thirty days after the expiration of the time specified, the Comptroller of the Currency shall have power to sell the bonds pledged for the circulation of said bank, at public auction in New York City, and, after providing for the redemption and cancellation of said circulation, and the necessary expenses of the sale, to pay over any balance remaining to the bank or its legal representative.

Re-assignment of bonds to closed banks.

Notes to be redeemed at Treasury.

Proceedings when association fails to deposit lawful money. See act of Feb. 18, 1875, correcting Rev. State., page 63.

104. (SEC. 5225.) Whenever the Treasurer has redeemed any of the notes of an association which has commenced to close its affairs under the six [five] preceding sections, he shall cause the notes to be mutilated and charged to the redemption account of the association; and all notes so redeemed by the Treasurer shall, every three months, be certified to and burned in the manner prescribed in section fifty-one hundred and eighty-four.

Destruction of redeemed notes. See act of June 23, 1874, page 59.

105. (SEC. 5226.) Whenever any national banking association fails to redeem in the lawful money of the United States any of its circulating notes, upon demand of payment duly made during the usual hours of business, at the office of such association, or at its designated place of redemption, the holder may cause the same to be protested, in one package by a notary public, unless the president or cashier of the association whose notes are presented for payment, or the president or cashier of the association at the place at which they are redeemable offers to waive demand and notice of the protest, and, in pursuance of such offer, makes, signs, and delivers to the party making such demand an admission in writing, stating the time of the demand, the amount demanded, and the fact of the non-payment thereof. The

Mode of protesting notes.

See act of June 20, 1874. section 8, page 56.

notary public, on making such protest, or upon receiving such admission, shall forthwith forward such admission or notice of protest to the Comptroller of the Currency, retaining a copy thereof. If, however, satisfactory proof is produced to the notary public that the payment of the notes demanded is restrained by order of any court of competent jurisdiction, he shall not protest the same. When the holder of any notes causes more than one note or package to be protested on the same day, he shall not receive pay for more than one protest.

One protest fee only on same day.

106. (SEC. 5227.) On receiving notice that any national banking association has failed to redeem any of its circulating notes, as specified in the preceding section, the Comptroller of the Currency, with the concurrence of the Secretary of the Treasury, may appoint a special agent, of whose appointment immediate notice shall be given to such association, who shall immediately proceed to ascertain whether it has refused to pay its circulating notes in the lawful money of the United States, when demanded, and shall report to the Comptroller the fact so ascertained. If from such protest, and the report so made, the Comptroller is satisfied that such association has refused to pay its circulating notes and is in default, he shall, within thirty days after he has received notice of such failure, declare the bonds deposited by such association forfeited to the United States, and they shall thereupon be so forfeited.

Examination by special agent, after notice of protest.

Forfeiture of bonds.

107. (SEC. 5228.) After a default on the part of an association to pay any of its circulating notes has been ascertained by the Comptroller, and notice thereof has been given by him to the association, it shall not be lawful for the association suffering the same to pay out any of its notes, discount any notes or bills, or otherwise prosecute the business of banking, except to receive and safely keep money belonging to it, and to deliver special deposits.

Association not to do business after notice of protest.

See act of Feb. 18, 1875, correcting Rev. Stats., page 63.

108. (SEC. 5229.) Immediately upon declaring the bonds of an association forfeited for non-payment of its notes, the Comptroller shall give notice, in such manner as the Secretary of the Treasury shall, by general rules or otherwise, direct, to the holders of the circulating notes of such association, to present them for payment at the Treasury of the United States; and the same shall be paid as presented in lawful money of the United States; whereupon the Comp-

Notice to note-holders.

Redemption of notes at Treasury, and cancellation of bonds.

troller may, in his discretion, cancel an amount of bonds pledged by such association equal at current market rates, not exceeding par, to the notes paid.

109. (SEC. 5230.) Whenever the Comptroller has become satisfied, by the protest or the waiver and admission specified in section fifty-two hundred and twenty-six, or by the report provided for in section fifty-two hundred and twenty-seven, that any association has refused to pay its circulating notes, he may, instead of canceling its bonds, cause so much of them as may be necessary to redeem its outstanding notes to be sold at public auction in the city of New York, after giving thirty days' notice of such sale to the association. For any deficiency in the proceeds of all the bonds of an association, when thus sold, to re-imburse to the United States the amount expended in paying the circulating notes of the association, the United States shall have a paramount lien upon all its assets; and such deficiency shall be made good out of such assets in preference to any and all other claims whatsoever, except the necessary costs and expenses of administering the same. *Sale of bonds at auction.* *The United States to have a paramount lien upon assets of associations.*

110. (SEC. 5231.) The Comptroller may, if he deems it for the interest of the United States, sell at private sale any of the bonds of an association shown to have made default in paying its notes, and receive therefor either money or the circulating notes of the association. But no such bonds shall be sold by private sale for less than par, nor for less than the market-value thereof at the time of sale; and no sales of any such bonds, either public or private, shall be complete until the transfer of the bonds shall have been made with the formalities prescribed by sections fifty-one hundred and sixty-two, fifty-one hundred and sixty-three, and fifty-one hundred and sixty-four. *Sale of bonds at private sale.* *Transfer of bonds sold.*

111. (SEC. 5232.) The Secretary of the Treasury may, from time to time, make such regulations respecting the disposition to be made of circulating notes after presentation at the Treasury of the United States for payment, and respecting the perpetuation of the evidence of the payment thereof, as may seem to him proper. *Disposition to be made of notes redeemed by Treasurer.*

112. (SEC. 5233.) All notes of national banking associations presented at the Treasury of the United States for payment shall, on being paid, be canceled. *Cancellation of notes.* *See act of June 20, 1874, section 3, page 55.*

Appointment
and duties of re-
ceivers.

Kennedy vs.
Gibson. 8 Wall.,
498; Bank of
Bethel vs. Pah-
quioque Bank, 14
Wall., 383; Bank
vs. Kennedy, 16
Wall., 19; in re.
Platt, Receiver,
&c., 1 Ben., 534.

113. (SEC. 5234.) On becoming satisfied, as specified in sections fifty-two hundred and twenty-six and fifty-two hundred and twenty-seven, that any association has refused to pay its circulating notes as therein mentioned, and is in default, the Comptroller of the Currency may forthwith appoint a receiver, and require of him such bond and security as he deems proper. Such receiver, under the direction of the Comptroller, shall take possession of the books, records, and assets of every description of such association, collect all debts, dues, and claims belonging to it, and, upon the order of a court of record of competent jurisdic-

See section 1,
act June 30, 1876,
page 66.

tion, may sell or compound all bad or doubtful debts, and, on a like order, may sell all the real and personal property of such association, on such terms as the court shall direct; and may, if necessary to pay the debts of such association, enforce the individual liability of the stockholders. Such receiver shall pay over all money so made to the Treasurer of the United States, subject to the order of the Comptroller, and also make report to the Comptroller of all his acts and proceedings.

Notice by
Comptroller to
creditors.

114. (SEC. 5235.) The Comptroller shall, upon appointing a receiver, cause notice to be given, by advertisement in such newspapers as he may direct, for three consecutive months, calling on all persons who may have claims against such association to present the same, and to make legal proof thereof.

Dividends by
Comptroller to
creditors.

Bank of Bethel
vs. Pahquioque
Bank, 14 Wall.,
383.

115. (SEC. 5236.) From time to time, after full provision has been first made for refunding to the United States any deficiency in redeeming the notes of such association, the Comptroller shall make a ratable dividend of the money so paid over to him by such receiver on all such claims as may have been proved to his satisfaction or adjudicated in a court of competent jurisdiction, and, as the proceeds of the assets of such association are paid over to him, shall make further dividends on all claims previously proved or adjudicated; and the remainder of the proceeds, if any, shall be paid over to the shareholders of such association, or their legal representatives, in proportion to the stock by them respectively held.

Injunction upon
receivership.

See sec. 736, p.
61.

116. (SEC. 5237.) Whenever an association against which procedings have been instituted, on account of any alleged refusal to redeem its circulating notes as aforesaid, denies having failed to do so, it may, at any time within ten days

41

after it has been notified of the appointment of an agent, as provided in section fifty-two hundred and twenty-seven, apply to the nearest circuit, or district, or territorial court of the United States to enjoin further proceedings in the premises; and such court, after citing the Comptroller of the Currency to show cause why further proceedings should not be enjoined, and after the decision of the court or finding of a jury that such association has not refused to redeem its circulating notes, when legally presented, in the lawful money of the United States, shall make an order enjoining the Comptroller, and any receiver acting under his direction, from all further proceedings on account of such alleged refusal.

117. (SEC. 5238.) All fees for protesting the notes issued by any national banking association shall be paid by the person procuring the protest to be made, and such association shall be liable therefor; but no part of the bonds deposited by such association shall be applied to the payment of such fees. All expenses of any preliminary or other examinations into the condition of any association shall be paid by such association. All expenses of any receivership shall be paid out of the assets of such association before distribution of the proceeds thereof. *Fees and expenses of protest and receivership.*

118. (SEC. 5239.) If the directors of any national banking association shall knowingly violate, or knowingly permit any of the officers, agents, or servants of the association to violate any of the provisions of this Title, all the rights, privileges, and franchises of the association shall be thereby forfeited. Such violation shall, however, be determined and adjudged by a proper circuit, district, or territorial court of the United States, in a suit brought for that purpose by the Comptroller of the Currency, in his own name, before the association shall be declared dissolved. And in cases of such violation, every director who participated in or assented to the same shall be held liable in his personal and individual capacity for all damages which the association, its shareholders, or any other person, shall have sustained in consequence of such violation. *Penalty for violation of provisions of this Title. Violation, how determined. Liability of directors for violation. Sections 5240, 5241, pages 34, 35.*

119. (SEC. 5242.)* All transfers of the notes, bonds, bills of exchange, or other evidences of debt owing to any national banking association, or of deposits to its credit; all assignments of mortgages, sureties on real estate, or of judg- *Transfers, assignments, &c., after an act of insolvency, void.*

*For part of section 5242 see page 51, under head of Suits and Jurisdiction.

ments or decrees in its favor; all deposits of money, bullion, or other valuable thing for its use, or for the use of any of its shareholders or creditors; and all payments of money to either, made after the commission of an act of insolvency, or in contemplation thereof, made with a view to prevent the application of its assets in the manner prescribed by this chapter, or with a view to the preference of one creditor to another, except in payment of its circulating notes, shall be utterly null and void.

CHAPTER SIX.

TAX ON UNAUTHORIZED CIRCULATION.

Capital of State bank converted into national association. 120. (SEC. 3410.) The capital of any State bank or banking association which has ceased or shall cease to exist, or which has been or shall be converted into a national bank, shall be assumed to be the capital as it existed immediately before such bank ceased to exist or was converted as aforesaid.

Circulation, when exempted from tax.

See act of July 12, 1882, sections 6 and 8, pages 73 and 74. 121. (SEC. 3411.) Whenever the outstanding circulation of any bank, association, corporation, company, or person is reduced to an amount not exceeding five per centum of the chartered or declared capital existing at the time the same was issued, said circulation shall be free from taxation; and whenever any bank which has ceased to issue notes for circulation, deposits in the Treasury of the United States, in lawful money, the amount of its outstanding circulation, to be redeemed at par, under such regulations as the Secretary of the Treasury shall prescribe, it shall be exempt from any tax upon such circulation.

Tax on notes of persons or State banks, used for circulation.

See act of Feb. 8, 1875, secs. 19 and 20, pages 61 and 62. 122. (SEC. 3412.) Every national banking association, State bank, or State banking association, shall pay a tax of ten per centum on the amount of notes of any person, or of any State bank or State banking association, used for circulation and paid out by them.

Tax on notes of towns, cities, &c., used for circulation.

See act of Feb. 8, 1875, secs. 19 & 20, pp. 61 and 62. 123. (SEC. 3413.) Every national banking association, State bank, or banker, or association, shall pay a tax of ten per centum on the amount of notes of any town, city, or municipal corporation, paid out by them.

Monthly returns of notes of persons, cities, State banks, &c., paid out.

See act of Feb. 8, 1875, page 62. 124. (SEC. 3414.) A true and complete return of the monthly amount of circulation, of deposits, and of capital, as aforesaid, and of the monthly amount of notes of persons town, city, or municipal corporation, State banks, or State banking associations paid out as aforesaid for the previous six months, shall be made and rendered in duplicate on the first day of December and the first day of June, by each of such banks, associations, corporations, companies, or persons, with a declaration annexed thereto, under the oath of such person, or of the president or cashier of such bank, association, corporation, or company, in such form and manner as may be prescribed by the Commissioner of Internal Revenue, that the same contains a true and faithful statement of the amounts subject to tax, as aforesaid; and one copy shall be transmitted to the collector of the district in which any such bank, association, corporation, or company is situated, or in which such person has his place of business, and one copy to the Commissioner of Internal Revenue.

125. (SEC. 3415.) In default of the returns provided in the preceding section, the amount of circulation, deposit, capital, and notes of persons, town, city, and municipal corporations, State banks, and State banking associations paid out, as aforesaid, shall be estimated by the Commissioner of Internal Revenue, upon the best information he can obtain. And for any refusal or neglect to make return and payment, any such bank, association, corporation, company, or person so in default shall pay a penalty of two hundred dollars, besides the additional penalty and forfeitures provided in other cases. *In default of returns, Commissioner to estimate.*

126. (SEC. 3416.) Whenever any State bank or banking association has been converted into a national banking association, and such national banking association has assumed the liabilities of such State bank or banking association, including the redemption of its bills, by any agreement or understanding whatever with the representatives of such State bank or banking association, such national banking association shall be held to make the required return and payment on the circulation outstanding, so long as such circulation shall exceed five per centum of the capital before such conversion of such State bank or banking association. *National bank to make return and payment of tax of converted State bank.*

127. (SEC. 3417.) The provisions of this chapter, relating to the tax on the deposits, capital, and circulation of banks, and to their returns, except as contained in sections thirty-four hundred and ten, thirty-four hundred and eleven, thirty-four hundred and twelve, thirty-four hundred and thirteen, *Provisions for tax on deposits, capital and circulation, not to apply to national banks. See act Feb. 18, 1875, correcting Rev. Stat., p. 62.*

44

and thirty-four hundred and sixteen, and such parts of sections thirty-four hundred and fourteen and thirty-four hundred and fifteen as relate to the tax of ten per centum on certain notes, shall not apply to associations which are taxed under and by virtue of Title "NATIONAL BANKS."

Section 3418, page 44.

United States securities exempt from local taxation.
Bank vs. Supervisors, 7 Wall., 26.

128. (SEC. 3701.) All stocks, bonds, Treasury notes, and other obligations of the United States, shall be exempt from taxation by or under State or municipal or local authority.*

CHAPTER SEVEN.

STAMP-TAX ON BANK-CHECKS.

Tax on bank-checks.
See act of Feb. 8, 1875, section 15, page 61.

129. (SEC. 3418.) There shall be levied, collected, and paid for and in respect of every bank-check, draft, or order for the payment of money, drawn upon any bank, banker, or trust company, at sight or on demand, by any person who makes, signs, or issues the same, or for whose use or benefit the same is made, signed or issued, two cents.

Official checks exempt from tax.

130. (SEC. 3420.) All bank-checks, drafts, or orders, as aforesaid, issued by the officers of the United States Government, or by officers of any State, county, town, or other municipal corporation, are exempt from taxation: *Provided*, That it is the intent hereby to exempt from liability to taxation such State, county, town, or other municipal corporations in the exercise only of functions strictly belonging to them in their ordinary governmental and municipal capacity.

Unstamped checks not admissible in evidence.

131. (SEC. 3421.) No bank-check, draft, or order, required by law to be stamped, which is issued without being duly stamped, nor any copy thereof, shall be admitted or used in evidence in any court until a legal stamp, denoting the amount of tax, is affixed thereto, as prescribed by law.*

Penalty for failure to stamp check.

132. (SEC. 3422.) Any person or persons who shall make, sign, or issue, or who shall cause to be made, signed, or issued, any instrument, document, or paper of any kind or description whatsoever, or shall accept, negotiate, or pay, or cause to be accepted, negotiated, or paid, any draft, or order, for the payment of money, without the same being duly stamped, or having thereupon an adhesive stamp for denoting the tax chargeable thereon, and canceled in the manner required by law, with intent to evade the provisions of this

* See also, in this connection, section 5413, on page 47.

Title, shall, for every such offense, forfeit the sum of fifty dollars, and such instrument, document, or paper, draft, [or] order, not being stamped according to law, shall be deemed invalid and of no effect: *Provided*, That hereafter, in all cases where the party has not affixed to any instrument the stamp required by law thereon, at the time of making or issuing the said instrument, and he or they, or any party having an interest therein, shall be subsequently desirous of affixing such stamp to said instrument, or, if said instrument be lost, to a copy thereof, he or they shall appear before the collector of the revenue of the proper district, who shall, upon the payment of the price of the proper stamp required by law, and of a penalty of double the amount of tax remaining unpaid, but in no case less than five dollars, and where the whole amount of the tax denoted by the stamp required shall exceed the sum of fifty dollars, on payment also of interest, at the rate of six per centum on said tax from the day on which such stamp ought to have been affixed, affix the proper stamp to such instrument or copy, and note upon the margin thereof the date of his so doing, and the fact that such penalty has been paid; and the same shall thereupon be deemed and held to be as valid, to all intents and purposes, as if stamped when made or issued. * *

Stamp may be subsequently affixed by collector. See act of June 23, 1874, and of Feb. 18, 1875, correcting Rev.Stat. p. 65.

133. (SEC. 3423.) In all cases where an adhesive stamp is used for denoting any tax imposed under this chapter, except as hereinafter provided, the person using or affixing the same shall write thereon the initials of his name and the date on which such stamp is attached or used, so that it may not again be used. And every person who fraudulently makes use of an adhesive stamp to denote any tax imposed by this chapter without so effectually canceling and obliterating such stamp, except as before mentioned, shall forfeit the sum of fifty dollars. * *

Stamps to be canceled.

Penalty for fraudulent use.

134. (SEC. 3424.) The Commissioner of Internal Revenue is authorized to prescribe such method for the cancellation of stamps as substitute for, or in addition to the method prescribed in this chapter, as he may deem expedient and effectual. * *

Method of cancellation.

CHAPTER EIGHT.

CRIMES AND MISDEMEANORS.

Penalty for unlawfully countersigning or delivering circulating notes. 135. (SEC. 5187.) No officer acting under the provisions of this Title shall countersign or deliver to any association, or to any other company or person, any circulating notes contemplated by this Title, except in accordance with the true intent and meaning of its provisions. Every officer who violates this section shall be deemed guilty of a high misdemeanor, and shall be fined not more than double the amount so countersigned and delivered, and imprisoned not less than one year and not more than fifteen years.

Penalty for offering or receiving United States or national-bank notes as security for loan, &c. 136. (SEC. 5207.) No association shall hereafter offer or receive United States notes or national-bank notes as security or as collateral security for any loan of money, or for a consideration agree to withhold the same from use, or offer or receive the custody or promise of custody of such notes as security, or as collateral security, or consideration for any loan of money. Any association offending against the provisions of this section shall be deemed guilty of a misdemeanor, and shall be fined not more than one thousand dollars and a further sum equal to one-third of the money so loaned. The officer or officers of any association who shall make any such loan shall be liable for a further sum equal to one-quarter of the money loaned; and any fine or penalty incurred by a violation of this section shall be recoverable for the benefit of the party bringing such suit.

Penalty for embezzlement. 137. (SEC. 5209.) Every president, director, cashier, teller, clerk, or agent of any association, who embezzles, abstracts, or willfully misapplies any of the moneys, funds, or credits of the association; or who, without authority from the directors, issues or puts in circulation any of the notes of the association; or who, without such authority, issues or puts forth any certificate of deposit, draws any order or bill of exchange, makes any acceptance, assigns any note, bond, draft, bill of exchange, mortgage, judgment, or decree; or who makes any false entry in any book, report, or statement of the association, with intent, in either case, to injure or defraud the association or any other company, body politic or corporate, or any individual person, or to deceive any officer of the association, or any agent appointed to examine the

affairs of any such association; and every person who with
like intent aids or abets any officer, clerk, or agent in any
violation of this section, shall be deemed guilty of a misdemeanor, and shall be imprisoned not less than five years nor
more than ten.

138. (SEC. 5413.) The words "obligation or other security
of the United States" shall be held to mean all bonds, certificates of indebtedness, national-bank currency, coupons,
United States notes, Treasury notes, fractional notes, certificates of deposit, bills, checks, or drafts for money, drawn
by or upon authorized officers of the United States, stamps
and other representatives of value, of whatever denomination, which have been or may [be] issued under any act of
Congress.

Obligations or
other securities
of the United
States defined.
See act of Feb.
18, 1875, page 63,
correcting Rev.
Stat.

139. (SEC. 5415.) Every person who falsely makes, forges,
or counterfeits, or causes or procures to be made, forged, or
counterfeited, or willingly aids or assists in falsely making,
forging, or counterfeiting, any note in imitation of, or purporting to be in imitation of, the circulating notes, issued by
any banking association now or hereafter authorized and
acting under the laws of the United States; or who passes,
utters, or publishes, or attempts to pass, utter, or publish,
any false, forged, or counterfeited note, purporting to be
issued by any such association doing a banking business,
knowing the same to be falsely made, forged, or counterfeited, or who falsely alters, or causes or procures to be
falsely altered, or willingly aids or assists in falsely altering
any such circulating notes, or passes, utters, or publishes,
or attempts to pass, utter, or publish as true, any falsely
altered or spurious circulating note issued, or purporting to
have been issued, by any such banking association, knowing the same to be falsely altered or spurious, shall be imprisoned at hard labor not less than five years nor more than
fifteen years, and fined not more than one thousand dollars.

Penalty for
counterfeiting
national-bank
notes.

140. (SEC. 5430.) Every person having control, custody,
or possession of any plate, or any part thereof, from which
has been printed, or which may be prepared by direction of
the Secretary of the Treasury for the purpose of printing,
any obligation or other security of the United States, who
uses such plate, or knowingly suffers the same to be used
for the purpose of printing any such or similar obligation, or
other security, or any part thereof, except as may be printed
or the use of the United States by order of the proper offi-

Penalty for
using plates to
print notes with-
out authority.

48

cer thereof; and every person who engraves, or causes or procures to be engraved, or assists in engraving, any plate in the likeness of any plate designed for the printing of such obligation or other security, or who sells any such plate, or who brings into the United States from any foreign place any such plate, except under the direction of the Secretary of the Treasury or other proper officer, or with any other intent, in either case, than that such plate be used for the printing of the obligations or other securities of the United States; or who has in his control, custody, or possession any metallic plate engraved after the similitude of any plate from which any such obligation or other security has been printed, with intent to use such plate, or suffer the same to be used in forging or counterfeiting any such obligation or other security, or any part thereof; or who has in his possession or custody, except under authority from the Secretary of the Treasury or other proper officer, any obligation or other security, engraved and printed after the similitude of any obligation or other security issued under the authority of the United States, with intent to sell or otherwise use the same; and every person who prints, photographs, or in any other manner makes or executes, or causes to be printed, photographed, made, or executed, or aids in printing, photographing, making, or executing any engraving, photograph, print, or impression in the likeness of any such obligation or other security, or any part thereof, or who sells any such engraving, photograph, print, or impression, except to the United States, or who brings into the United States from any foreign place any such engraving, photograph, print, or impression, except by direction of some proper officer of the United States, or who has or retains in his control or possession, after a distinctive paper has been adopted by the Secretary of the Treasury for the obligations and other securities of the United States, any similar paper adapted to the making of any such obligation or other security, except under the authority of the Secretary of the Treasury or some other proper officer of the United States, shall be punished by a fine of not more than five thousand dollars, or by imprisonment at hard labor not more than fifteen years, or by both.

141. (SEC. 5431.) Every person who, with intent to defraud, passes, utters, publishes, or sells, or attempts to pass, utter, publish, or sell, or brings into the United States with

intent to pass, publish, utter, or sell, or keeps in possession
or conceals with like intent any falsely made, forged, counterfeited, or altered obligation, or other security of the United
States, shall be punished by a fine of not more than five
thousand dollars, and by imprisonment at hard labor not
more than fifteen years.

142. (SEC. 5432.) Every person who, without authority *Penalty for taking impression of tools, implements, &c.* from the United States, takes, procures, or makes, upon lead,
foil, wax, plaster, paper, or any other substance or material,
an impression, stamp, or imprint of, from, or by the use of
any bed-plate, bed-piece, die, roll, plate, seal, type, or other
tool, implement, instrument, or thing used or fitted or intended to be used, in printing, stamping, or impressing, or
in making other tools, implements, instruments, or things,
to be used, or fitted or intended to be used, in printing,
stamping, or impressing any kind or description of obligation or other security of the United States, now authorized
or hereafter to be authorized by the United States, or circulating note or evidence of debt of any banking association
under the laws thereof, shall be punished by imprisonment
at hard labor not more than ten years, or by a fine of not
more than five thousand dollars, or both.

143. (SEC. 5433.) Every person who, with intent to de- *.Penalty for having in posses- sion impression of tools, imple- ments, &c.* fraud, has in his possession, keeping, custody, or control,
without authority from the United States, any imprint,
stamp, or impression, taken or made upon any substance
or material whatsoever, of any tool, implement, instrument,
or thing, used, or fitted or intended to be used, for any of the
purposes mentioned in the preceding section; or who, with
intent to defraud, sells, gives, or delivers any such imprint,
stamp, or impression to any other person, shall be punished
by imprisonment at hard labor not more than ten years, or
by a fine of not more than five thousand dollars.

144. (SEC. 5434.) Every person who buys, sells, exchanges, *Penalty for buying, selling, or dealing in forged or altered notes.* transfers, receives, or delivers, any false, forged, counterfeited, or altered obligation or other security of the United
States, or circulating note of any banking association organized or acting under the laws thereof, which has been or
may hereafter be issued by virtue of any act of Congress,
with the intent that the same be passed, published, or
used as true and genuine, shall be imprisoned at hard labor
not more than ten years, or fined not more than five thousand dollars, or both.

145. (SEC. 5437.) In all cases where the charter of any
corporation which has been or may be created by act of Congress has expired or may hereafter expire, if any director,
officer, or agent of the corporation, or any trustee thereof,
or any agent of such trustee, or any person having in his
possession or under his control the property of the corporation for the purpose of paying or redeeming its notes and
obligations, knowingly issues, re-issues, or utters as money,
or in any other way knowingly puts in circulation any bill,
note, check, draft, or other security purporting to have been
made by any such corporation whose charter has expired,
or by any officer thereof, or purporting to have been made
under authority derived therefrom, or if any person knowingly aids in any such act, he shall be punished by a fine of
not more than ten thousand dollars, or by imprisonment not
less than one year nor more than five years, or by both such
fine and imprisonment. But nothing herein shall be construed to make it unlawful for any person, not being such
director, officer, or agent of the corporation, or any trustee
thereof, or any agent of such trustee, or any person having
in his possession or under his control the property of the
corporation for the purpose hereinbefore set forth, who has
received or may hereafter receive such bill, note, check, draft,
or other security, bona fide and in the ordinary transactions of
business, to utter as money or otherwise circulate the same.

Marginal notes: Penalty for unlawfully putting in circulation the notes, drafts, &c., of closed associations. Persons not officers or agents of closed associations may circulate the notes of such associations.

CHAPTER NINE.

* SUITS, JURISDICTION, AND EVIDENCE.

146. (SEC. 563.) The district courts shall have jurisdiction as follows:

Marginal note: Jurisdiction of district courts.

* * * * * *

Fifteenth. Of all suits by or against any association established under any law providing for national banking associations within the district for which the court is held.

Marginal note: Suits by or against national banks. Kennedy vs. Gibson, 8 Wall., 506.

* * * * * *

147. (SEC. 629.) The circuit courts shall have original jurisdiction as follows:

Marginal note: Jurisdiction of circuit courts.

* * * * * *

Tenth. Of all suits by or against any banking association
established in the district for which the court is held, under
any law providing for national banking associations.

Marginal note: Suits by or against national banks. Kennedy vs. Gibson, 8 Wall., 506.

_____

* Jurisdiction of courts amended by proviso in section 4 of act July 12, 1882, page 72.

Eleventh. Of all suits brought by any banking association established in the district for which the court is held, under the provisions of title "THE NATIONAL BANKS," to enjoin the Comptroller of the Currency, or any receiver acting under his direction, as provided by said title. Suits by national banks to enjoin Comptroller or receiver. See act of Feb. 18, 1875, correcting Rev. Stat., page 63.

* * * * * *

148. (SEC. 711.) The jurisdiction vested in the courts of the United States, in the cases and proceedings hereinafter mentioned, shall be exclusive of the courts of the several States: Exclusive jurisdiction of United States courts.

* * * * * *

Second. Of all suits for penalties and forfeitures incurred under the laws of the United States. Suits for penalties and forfeitures.

* * * * * *

149. (SEC. 5198.)* Suits, actions, and proceedings against any association under this Title may be had in any circuit, district, or territorial court of the United States held within the district in which such association may be established, or in any State, county, or municipal court in the county or city in which said association is located, having jurisdiction in similar cases. In what courts an its may be brought. See act of Feb. 18, 1875, correcting Rev. Stat., page 63.

150. (SEC. 5242.)* No attachment, injunction, or execution shall be issued against such association or its property before final judgment in any suit, action, or proceeding, in any State, county, or municipal court. Attachment not to issue before final judgment in State court.

151. (SEC. 736.) All proceedings by any national banking association to enjoin the Comptroller of the Currency, under the provisions of any law relating to national banking associations, shall be had in the district where such association is located. Proceedings to enjoin Comptroller, where had. See sec. 5237, p. 40.

152. (SEC. 380.) All suits and proceedings arising out of the provisions of law governing national banking associations, in which the United States or any of its officers or agents shall be parties, shall be conducted by the district attorneys of the several districts under the direction and supervision of the Solicitor of the Treasury. U. S. district attorney to conduct suits, under supervision of Solicitor of Treasury.

153. (SEC. 884.) Every certificate, assignment, and conveyance executed by the Comptroller of the Currency, in pursuance of law, and sealed with his seal of office, shall be received in evidence in all places and courts; and all copies of papers in his office, certified by him and authenticated by Instruments and copies, certified and sealed by Comptroller, may be evidence.

---

* For parts of sections 5198 and 5242 see also pages 29 and 41.

the said seal, shall in all cases be evidence equally with the originals. An impression of such seal directly on the paper shall be as valid as if made on wax or wafer.

Certified copies of organization certificate may be evidence.

154. (SEC. 885.) Copies of the organization certificate of any national banking association, duly certified by the Comptroller of the Currency, and authenticated by his seal of office, shall be evidence in all courts and places within the jurisdiction of the United States of the existence of the association, and of every matter which could be proved by the production of the original certificate.

AMENDMENTS

AND

ADDITIONAL ACTS,

1874-'82.

AMENDMENTS AND ADDITIONAL ACTS.

AN ACT

Fixing the amount of United States notes, providing for a redistribution of national-bank currency, and for other purposes.

Be it enacted by the Senate and House of Representatives of the United States of America in Congress assembled, That the act entitled "An act to provide a national currency secured by a pledge of United States bonds, and to provide for the circulation and redemption thereof," approved June third, eighteen hundred and sixty-four, shall hereafter be known as the "national-bank act." **"The National-Bank Act."**

SEC. 2. That section thirty-one of the "national-bank act" be so amended that the several associations therein provided for shall not hereafter be required to keep on hand any amount of money whatever by reason of the amount of their respective circulations; but the moneys required by said section to be kept at all times on hand shall be determined by the amount of deposits in all respects, as provided for in the said section. **Lawful money reserve on circulation abolished, except as to national gold-banks. See sec. 5191, p. 26.**

SEC. 3. That every association organized, or to be organized, under the provisions of the said act, and of the several acts amendatory thereof, shall at all times keep and have on deposit in the Treasury of the United States, in lawful money of the United States, a sum equal to five per centum of its circulation, to be held and used for the redemption of such circulation; which sum shall be counted as a part of its lawful reserve, as provided in section two of this act; and when the circulating notes of any such associations, assorted or unassorted, shall be presented for redemption, in sums of one thousand dollars or any multiple thereof, to the Treasurer of the United States, the same shall be redeemed in United States notes. All notes so redeemed shall be charged by the Treasurer of the United States to the respective associations issuing the same, and he shall notify them severally, on the first day of each month, or oftener, at his discretion, of the amount of such redemp- **Redemption fund to be deposited with Treasurer.** **May be counted as lawful reserve.** **Provisions relative to redemption of notes by Treasurer.**

(55)

tions; and whenever such redemptions for any association shall amount to the sum of five hundred dollars, such association so notified shall forthwith deposit with the Treasurer of the United States a sum in United States notes equal to the amount of its circulating notes so redeemed. And all notes of national banks, worn, defaced, mutilated, or otherwise unfit for circulation, shall, when received by any assistant treasurer or at any designated depository of the United States, be forwarded to the Treasurer of the United States for redemption as provided herein. And when such redemptions have been so reimbursed, the circulating notes so redeemed shall be forwarded to the respective associations by which they were issued; but if any of such notes are worn, mutilated, defaced, or rendered otherwise unfit for use, they shall be forwarded to the Comptroller of the Currency and destroyed, and replaced as now provided by law: *Provided,* That each of said associations shall reimburse to the Treasury the charges for transportation, and the costs for assorting such notes; and the associations hereafter organized shall also severally reimburse to the Treasury the cost of engraving such plates as shall be ordered by each association respectively; and the amount assessed upon each association shall be in proportion to the circulation redeemed, and be charged to the fund on deposit with the Treasurer: *And provided further,* That so much of section thirty-two of said national-bank act requiring or permitting the redemption of its circulating notes elsewhere than at its own counter, except as provided for in this section, is hereby repealed.

SEC. 4. That any association organized under this act, or any of the acts of which this is an amendment, desiring to withdraw its circulating notes, in whole or in part, may, upon the deposit of lawful money with the Treasurer of the United States in sums of not less than nine thousand dollars, take up the bonds which said association has on deposit with the Treasurer for the security of such circulating notes, which bonds shall be assigned to the bank in the manner specified in the nineteenth section of the national-bank act; and the outstanding notes of said association, to an amount equal to the legal-tender notes deposited, shall be redeemed at the Treasury of the United States, and destroyed as now provided by law: *Provided,* That the amount of the bonds on deposit for circulation shall not be reduced below fifty thousand dollars.

Mutilated notes to be returned by assistant treasurers.

Associations to reimburse the Treasury for cost of redemption, new plates, &c.

See act July 12, 1882, sec. 8, page 74.

Redemption agents in cities abolished.

See secs. 5192, 5195, and 5226, pp. 27, 28, and 37.

Provisions for retiring circulation and withdrawing bonds.

See sec. 5167, p. 19.

See act July 12, 1882, sec. 9, page 74.

Limit of withdrawal of bonds.

See secs. 5159, 5160, and 5167, pp. 17 and 20.

SEC. 5. That the Comptroller of the Currency shall, under such rules and regulations as the Secretary of the Treasury may prescribe, cause the charter numbers of the association to be printed upon all national-bank notes which may be hereafter issued by him. The charter number of banks to be printed upon their notes.

SEC. 6. That the amount of United States notes outstanding and to be used as a part of the circulating medium shall not exceed the sum of three hundred and eighty-two million dollars, which said sum shall appear in each monthly statement of the public debt, and no part thereof shall be held or used as a reserve. Maximum amount of U. S. notes outstanding.

SEC. 7. That so much of the act entitled "An act to provide for the redemption of the three per cent. temporary-loan certificates, and for an increase of national-bank notes," as provides that no circulation shall be withdrawn under the provisions of section 6 of said act, until after the fifty-four millions granted in section one of said act shall have been taken up, is hereby repealed; and it shall be the duty of the Comptroller of the Currency, under the direction of the Secretary of the Treasury, to proceed forthwith, and he is hereby authorized and required, from time to time, as applications shall be duly made therefor, and until the full amount of fifty-five million dollars shall be withdrawn, to make requisitions upon each of the national banks described in said section, and in the manner therein provided, organized in States having an excess of circulation, to withdraw and return so much of their circulation as by said act may be apportioned to be withdrawn from them, or, in lieu thereof, to deposit in the Treasury of the United States lawful money sufficient to redeem such circulation ; and upon the return of the circulation required, or the deposit of lawful money, as herein provided, a proportionate amount of the bonds held to secure the circulation of such association as shall make such return or deposit shall be surrendered to it. Provisions relative to withdrawal of $55,000,000 of circulation.
See sec. 5179, p. 22.
Superseded by act of Jan. 14, 1875, sec. 3, page 60.
Bonds to be returned to association in proportion to circulation withdrawn.

SEC. 8. That upon the failure of the national banks upon which requisition for circulation shall be made, or of any of them, to return the amount required, or to deposit in the Treasury lawful money to redeem the circulation required, within thirty days, the Comptroller of the Currency shall at once sell, as provided in section forty-nine of the national-currency act, approved June third, eighteen hundred and sixty-four, bonds held to secure the redemption of the circu- Bonds to be sold on failure of association to return circulation.
Superseded by act of Jan. 14, 1875, sec. 3, page 60.
See sec. 5231, p. 39.

lation of the association or associations which shall so fail, to an amount sufficient to redeem the circulation required of such association or associations, and with the proceeds, which shall be deposited in the Treasury of the United States, so much of the circulation of such association or associations shall be redeemed as will equal the amount required and not returned; and if there be an excess of proceeds over the amount required for such redemption, it shall be returned to the association or associations whose bonds shall have been sold. And it shall be the duty of the Treasurer, assistant treasurers, designated depositaries, and national bank depositaries of the United States, who shall be kept informed by the Comptroller of the Currency of such associations as shall fail to return circulation as required, to assort and return to the Treasury for redemption the notes of such associations as shall come into their hands until the amount required shall be redeemed, and in like manner to assort and return to the treasury, for redemption, the notes of such national banks as have failed, or gone into voluntary liquidation for the purpose of winding up their affairs, and of such as shall hereafter so fail or go into liquidation.

Assistant treasurers and depositaries to assort and return notes to Treasury.

SEC. 9. That from and after the passage of this act it shall be lawful for the Comptroller of the Currency, and he is hereby required, to issue circulating notes, without delay, as applications therefor are made, not to exceed the sum of fifty-five million dollars, to associations, organized, or to be organized, in those States and Territories having less than their proportion of circulation, under an apportionment made on the basis of population and of wealth, as shown by the returns of the census of eighteen hundred and seventy; and every association hereafter organized shall be subject to, and be governed by, the rules, restrictions, and limitations, and possess the rights, privileges, and franchises, now or hereafter to be prescribed by law as to national banking associations, with the same power to amend, alter, and repeal provided by "the national-bank act:" *Provided*, That the whole amount of circulation withdrawn and redeemed from banks transacting business shall not exceed fifty-five million dollars, and that such circulation shall be withdrawn and redeemed as it shall be necessary to supply the circulation previously issued to the banks in those States having less

Providing for the issue of new notes in place of $55,000,000 withdrawn. Superseded by act of Jan. 14, 1875, sec. 3, page 60.

New associations to be subject to national-bank act.

Provisos relative to withdrawal of circulation. Superseded by act of Jan. 14, 1875, sec. 3, page 60.

59

than their apportionment: *And provided further*, That
not more than thirty millions dollars shall be withdrawn and
redeemed as herein contemplated during the fiscal year ending June thirtieth, eighteen hundred and seventy-five.
Approved June 20, 1874.

EXTRACT FROM AN ACT

Making appropriations for sundry civil expenses of the Government for the fiscal year ending June 30, 1875.

For the maceration of national-bank notes, United States
notes, and other obligations of the United States authorized
to be destroyed, ten thousand dollars; and that all such
issues hereafter destroyed may be destroyed by maceration
instead of burning to ashes, as now provided by law; and
that so much of sections twenty-four and forty-three of the
national-currency act as requires national-bank notes to be
burned to ashes is hereby repealed.
Approved June 23, 1874.

Notes to bo destroyed by maceration instead of by burning. See secs. 5184 and 5225, pp. 24 and 37.

AN ACT

To provide for the resumption of specie payments.

*Be it enacted by the Senate and House of Representatives
of the United States of America in Congress assembled,* That
the Secretary of the Treasury is hereby authorized and required, as rapidly as practicable, to cause to be coined, at
the mints of the United States, silver coins of the denominations of ten, twenty-five, and fifty cents, of standard value,
and to issue them in redemption of an equal number and
amount of fractional currency of similar denominations, or,
at his discretion, he may issue such silver coins through the
mints, the sub-treasuries, public depositaries, and post-offices
of the United States; and, upon such issue, he is hereby
authorized and required to redeem an equal amount of such
fractional currency, until the whole amount of such fractional currency outstanding shall be redeemed.

Issue of silver coins for the redemption of fractional currency authorized.

SEC. 2. That so much of section three thousand five hundred and twenty-four of the Revised Statutes of the United States as provides for a charge of one-fifth of one per centum for converting standard gold bullion into coin is hereby repealed; and hereafter no charge shall be made for that service.

SEC. 3. That section five thousand one hundred and seventy-seven of the Revised Statutes, limiting the aggregate amount of circulating notes of national banking associations, be, and is hereby, repealed; and each existing banking association may increase its circulating notes in accordance with existing law without respect to said aggregate limit; and new banking associations may be organized in accordance with existing law without respect to said aggregate limit; and the provisions of law for the withdrawal and redistribution of national bank currency among the several States and Territories are hereby repealed. And whenever, and so often, as circulating notes shall be issued to any such banking association, so increasing its capital or circulating notes, or so newly organized as aforesaid, it shall be the duty of the Secretary of the Treasury to redeem the legal-tender United States notes in excess only of three hundred million of dollars, to the amount of eighty per centum of the sum of national-bank notes so issued to any such banking association as aforesaid, and to continue such redemption as such circulating notes are issued until there shall be outstanding the sum of three hundred million dollars of such legal-tender United States notes, and no more. And on and after the first day of January, anno Domini eighteen hundred and seventy-nine, the Secretary of the Treasury shall redeem, in coin, the United States legal-tender notes then outstanding, on their presentation for redemption at the office of the assistant treasurer of the United States in the city of New York, in sums of not less than fifty dollars. And to enable the Secretary of the Treasury to prepare and provide for the redemption in this act authorized or required, he is authorized to use any surplus revenues, from time to time, in the Treasury not otherwise appropriated, and to issue, sell, and dispose of, at not less than par, in coin, either of the descriptions of bonds of the United States described in the act of Congress approved July fourteenth, eighteen hundred and seventy, entitled "An act to authorize the

Margin notes:

Repeal of authority to charge a percentage for conversion of bullion into coin.

Repeal of provision limiting aggregate amo'nt of circulating notes.

See secs. 5177 to 5181, pages 22 and 23.

Repeal of provisions for withdrawal of currency.

See act of June 20, 1874, secs. 7, 8, and 9.

Redemption of legal-tenders, as national-bank notes are issued.

Legal-tenders not to be reduced below $300,000,000.

Subsequent act of May 31, 1878, forbid further retirement of legal tender notes and fixed limit at amount then outstanding, $346,681,016.

Coin redemption on and after Jan. 1, 1879.

Providing for coin redemption.

refunding of the national debt," with like qualities, privileges, and exemptions, to the extent necessary to carry this act into full effect, and to use the proceeds thereof for the purposes aforesaid. And all provisious of law inconsistent with the provisions of this act are hereby repealed.

Approved January 14, 1875.

AN ACT

To remove the limitation restricting the circulation of banking associations issuing notes payable in gold.

Be it enacted by the Senate and House of Representatives of the United States of America in Congress assembled, That so much of section five thousand one hundred and eighty-five of the Revised Statutes of the United States as limits the circulation of banking associations, organized for the purpose of issuing notes payable in gold, severally to one million dollars, be, and the same is hereby, repealed; and each of such existing banking associations may increase its circulating notes, and new banking associations may be organized, in accordance with existing law, without respect to such limitation.

Approved January 19, 1875.

Repeal of limit upon amount of circulation of national gold-banks.

See sec. 5185, p. 25.

EXTRACT FROM AN ACT

To amend existing customs and internal revenue laws, and for other purposes.

SEC. 15. That the words "bank-check, draft, or order for the payment of any sum of money whatsoever, drawn upon any bank, banker, or trust-company, at sight or on demand, two cents," in Schedule B of the act of June thirtieth, eighteen hundred and sixty-four, be, and the same is hereby, stricken out, and the following paragraph inserted in lieu thereof:

"Bank-check, draft, order, or voucher for the payment of any sum of money whatsoever, drawn upon any bank, banker, or trust-company, two cents."

Tax on bank-checks.

See sec. 3418, p. 44.

SEC. 19. That every person, firm, association other than national bank associations, and every corporation, State bank, or State banking association, shall pay a tax of ten

Tax on notes of persons or State banks paid out.

See secs. 3412 and 3413, p. 42.

per centum on the amount of their own notes used for circulation and paid out by them.

Tax on notes of persons, State banks, towns, cities, &c., used for circulation.

See secs, 3412 and 3413, p. 42.

SEC. 20. That every such person, firm, association, corporation, State bank, or State banking association, and also every national banking association, shall pay a like tax of ten per centum on the amount of notes of any person, firm, association other than a national banking association, or of any corporation, State bank, or State banking association, or of any town, city, or municipal corporation, used for circulation and paid out by them.

Returns to be made to the Commissioner of Internal Revenue.

See sec. 3414, 42.

SEC. 21. That the amount of such circulating notes, and of the tax due thereon, shall be returned, and the tax paid at the same time, and in the same manner, and with like penalties for failure to return and pay the same, as provided by law for the return and payment of taxes on deposits, capital, and circulation, imposed by the existing provisions of internal revenue law.

Approved February 8, 1875.

EXTRACTS FROM AN ACT

To correct errors and to supply omissions in the Revised Statutes of the United States.*

Be it enacted by the Senate and House of Representatives of the United States of America in Congress assembled, That for

Purpose of act.

the purpose of correcting errors and supplying omissions in the act entitled "An act to revise and consolidate the statutes of the United States in force on the first day of December, anno Domini one thousand eight hundred and seventy-three," so as to make the same truly express such laws, the following amendments are hereby made therein:

Seal of office of Comptroller.

Section three hundred and thirty is amended by adding thereto the following: "A description of the seal, with an impression thereof, and a certificate of approval by the Secretary of the Treasury, shall be filed in the Office of the Secretary of State."

Annual report of Comptroller.

Section three hundred and thirty-three is amended by inserting, after the word "Congress," in the second line, the words "at the commencement of its session."

* The corrections indicated have been made in the text.

63

Section six hundred and twenty-nine is amended by strik- Suits by banks.
ing out, in the first line of paragraph eleven, the words "or
against."

Section three thousand four hundred and seventeen is Tax on depos-
amended by inserting, in the fourth* line, after the word its, capital, and circulation.
"twelve," the words "thirty-four hundred and thirteen."

Section three thousand eight hundred and eleven is amend- Annual report
ed by striking out "Secretary of the Treasury," and insert- of Comptroller.
ing "Comptroller of the Currency;" also, by adding, after
the word "banks," in the second line, the words "and banks
under State and territorial laws."

Section five thousand one hundred and eighty-three is Post-notes pro-
amended by inserting, after the word "issue," in the second hibited.
line, the words "post-notes or."

Section five thousand one hundred and ninety-eight is Where suits
amended by adding thereto the following: "That suits, ac- against associations, and proceedings against any association under this tions may be had.
Title may be had in any circuit, district, or territorial court
of the United States held within the district in which such
association may be established, or in any State, county, or
municipal court in the county or city in which said association is located having jurisdiction in similar cases."

Section five thousand two hundred and twenty-four is Bonds of closed
amended by adding thereto the following: "And if any such banks to be sold for failure to de-
bank shall fail to make the deposit and take up its bonds posit legal-tender notes.
for thirty days after the expiration of the time specified, the
Comptroller of the Currency shall have power to sell the
bonds pledged for the circulation of said bank, at public auction in New York City, and, after providing for the redemption and cancellation of said circulation and the necessary
expenses of the sale, to pay over any balance remaining to
the bank or its legal representative."

Section five thousand two hundred and twenty-eight is Failure to re-
amended by striking out, in the third line, the words "of deem circulating notes.
forfeiture of the bonds," and inserting the word "thereof."

Section five thousand four hundred and thirteen is amended Defining nation-
by inserting, in the third line, after the word "national," the al currency.
word "bank."

Approved February 18, 1875.

---

* Fifth line of this compilation.

AN ACT

To amend section five thousand two hundred and forty of the Revised Statutes of the United States, in relation to compensation of national-bank examiners.*

Be it enacted by the Senate and House of Representatives of the United States of America in Congress assembled, That

Defining the compensation of national-bank examiners.
See page 35.

section five thousand two hundred and forty of the Revised Statutes of the United States be so amended that the latter clause of said section, after the word "Comptroller" in the eighth† line of said section, be amended so that the same shall read as follows, namely: "That all persons appointed to be examiners of national banks not located in the redemption-cities specified in section five thousand one hundred and ninety-two of the Revised Statutes of the United States, or in any one of the States of Oregon, California, and Nevada, or in the Territories, shall receive compensation for such examination as follows: For examining national banks having a capital less than one hundred thousand dollars, twenty dollars; those having a capital of one hundred thousand dollars and less than three hundred thousand dollars, twenty-five dollars; those having a capital of three hundred thousand dollars and less than four hundred thousand dollars, thirty-five dollars; those having a capital of four hundred thousand dollars and less than five hundred thousand dollars, forty dollars; those having a capital of five hundred thousand dollars and less than six hundred thousand dollars, fifty dollars; those having a capital of six hundred thousand dollars and over, seventy-five dollars; which amounts shall be assessed by the Comptroller of the Currency upon, and paid by, the respective associations so examined, and shall be in lieu of the compensation and mileage heretofore allowed for making said examinations; and per-

Compensation of examiners in certain cities, States, and Territories.

sons appointed to make examination of national banks in the cities named in section five thousand one hundred and ninety-two of the Revised Statutes of the United States, or in any one of the States of Oregon, California, and Nevada, or in the Territories, shall receive such compensation as may be fixed by the Secretary of the Treasury upon the recommendation of the Comptroller of the Currency; and the same shall be assessed and paid in the manner hereinbefore provided."

Approved February 19, 1875.

---

* This amendment has been incorporated into the text.
† Ninth line of this compilation.

AN ACT

To provide for the stamping of unstamped instruments, documents, or papers.

Be it enacted by the Senate and House of Representatives of the United States of America in Congress assembled, That all instruments, documents, and papers heretofore made, signed, or issued, and subject to a stamp-duty or tax under any law heretofore existing and remaining unstamped, may be stamped by any person having an interest therein, or, where the original is lost, a copy thereof, at any time prior to the first of January, eighteen hundred and seventy-six. And said instruments, documents, and papers, and any record thereof, shall be as valid, to all intents and purposes, as if stamped when made, signed or issued; but no right acquired in good faith shall in any manner be affected by such stamping as aforesaid: *Provided,* That to render such stamping valid, the person desiring to stamp the same shall appear with the instrument, document, or paper, or copy thereof, before some judge or clerk of a court of record, and before him affix the proper stamp; and the said judge or clerk shall indorse on such writing or copy a certificate, under his hand, when made by said judge, and under his hand and seal, when made by said clerk, setting forth the date at which, and the place where, the stamp was so affixed, the name of the person presenting said writing or copy, the fact that it was thus affixed, and that the stamp was duly canceled in his presence.

Stamps may be affixed to unstamped checks until January 1, 1876. See sec. 3422, p. 44.

By whom, and how, affixed.

SEC. 2. That all laws or parts of laws in conflict with the above are hereby repealed.

Repealing clause.

Approved June 23, 1874.

EXTRACT FROM AN ACT

To correct errors and supply omissions in the Revised Statutes of the United States.

Section three thousand four hundred and twenty-two is amended by inserting, after the word "issued," in the twenty-seventh* line, the following: *"And provided further,* That where it shall appear to said collector, upon oath or other-

Amending sec. 3422 of Rev. Stat., relative to unstamped instruments.

See p. 45.

---

* Thirty-second line of this compilation.

wise, to his satisfaction, that any such instrument has not been duly stamped at the time of making or issuing the same, by reason of accident, mistake, inadvertence, or urgent necessity, and without any willful design to defraud the United States of the stamps, or to evade or delay the payment thereof, then, and in such case, if such instrument, or, if the original be lost, a copy thereof, duly certified by the officer having charge of any records in which such original is required to be recorded, or otherwise duly proven to the satisfaction of the collector, shall, within twelve calendar months after the making or issuing thereof, be brought to the said collector of revenue to be stamped, and the stamp-tax chargeable thereon shall be paid, it shall be lawful for the said collector to remit the penalty aforesaid, and to cause such instrument to be duly stamped."

(Marginal note: Collector may affix stamp without penalty in certain cases.)

Approved February 18, 1875.

AN ACT

Authorizing the appointment of receivers of national banks, and for other purposes.

Be it enacted by the Senate and House of Representatives of the United States of America in Congress assembled, That whenever any national banking association shall be dissolved, and its rights, privileges, and franchises declared forfeited, as prescribed in section fifty-two hundred and thirty-nine of the Revised Statutes of the United States, or whenever any creditor of any national banking association shall have obtained a judgment against it in any court of record, and made application, accompanied by a certificate from the clerk of the court stating that such judgment has been rendered and has remained unpaid for the space of thirty days, or whenever the Comptroller shall become satisfied of the insolvency of a national banking association, he may, after due examination of its affairs, in either case, appoint a receiver, who shall proceed to close up such association, and enforce the personal liability of the shareholders, as provided in section fifty-two hundred and thirty-four of said statutes.

(Marginal note: Receiver may be appointed for any violation of law, or neglect to pay judgment, or in case of insolvency. See secs. 5234 and 5239, pp. 40 and 41.)

SEC. 2. That when any national banking association shall have gone into liquidation under the provisions of section five thousand two hundred and twenty of said statutes, the

(Marginal note: Individual liability of shareholders in case of liquidation, how enforced.)

individual liability of the shareholders provided for by section fifty-one hundred and fifty-one of said statutes may be enforced by any creditor of such association, by bill in equity in the nature of a creditor's bill, brought by such creditor on behalf of himself and of all other creditors of the association, against the shareholders thereof, in any court of the United States having original jurisdiction in equity for the district in which such association may have been located or established.

SEC. 3. That whenever any association shall have been or shall be placed in the hands of a receiver, as provided in section fifty-two hundred and thirty-four and other sections of said statutes, and when, as provided in section fifty-two hundred and thirty-six thereof, the Comptroller shall have paid to each and every creditor of such association, not including shareholders who are creditors of such association, whose claim or claims as such creditor shall have been proved, or allowed as therein prescribed, the full amount of such claims and all expenses of the receivership, and the redemption of the circulating notes of such association shall have been provided for by depositing lawful money of the United States with the Treasurer of the United States, the Comptroller of the Currency shall call a meeting of the shareholders of such association by giving notice thereof for thirty days in a newspaper published in the town, city, or county where the business of such association was carried on, or if no newspaper is there published, in the newspaper published nearest thereto, at which meeting the shareholders shall elect an agent, voting by ballot, in person or by proxy, each share of stock entitling the holder to one vote; and when such agent shall have received votes representing at least a majority of the stock in value and number of shares, and when any of the shareholders of the association shall have executed and filed a bond to the satisfaction of the Comptroller of the Currency, conditioned for the payment and discharge in full of any and every claim that may hereafter be proved and allowed against such association by and before a competent court, and for the faithful performance and discharge of all and singular the duties of such trust, the Comptroller and the receiver shall thereupon transfer and deliver to such agent all the undivided or uncollected or other assets and property of such association

When bank may elect agent to manage its affairs.

Meeting of shareholders to be called by Comptroller and public notice thereof to be given.

When assets of bank may be turned over to agent.

then remaining in the hands or subject to the order or control of said Comptroller and said receiver, or either of them; and for this purpose, said Comptroller and said receiver are hereby severally empowered to execute any deed, assignment, transfer, or other instrument in writing that may be necessary and proper; whereupon the said Comptroller and the said receiver shall, by virtue of this act, be discharged and released from any and all liabilities to such association, and to each and all of the creditors and shareholders thereof; and such agent is hereby authorized to sell, compromise, or compound the debts due to such association upon the order of a competent court of record or of the United States circuit court for the district where the business of the association was carried on. Such agent shall hold, control, and dispose of the assets and property of any association which he may receive as hereinbefore provided for the benefit of the shareholders of such association as they, or a majority of them in value or number of shares, may direct, distributing such assets and property among such shareholders in proportion to the shares held by each; and he may, in his own name or in the name of such association, sue and be sued, and do all other lawful acts and things necessary to finally settle and distribute the assets and property in his hands. In selecting an agent as hereinbefore provided, administrators or executors of deceased shareholders may act and sign as the decedent might have done if living, and guardians may so act and sign for their ward or wards.

Powers of agent.

Votes on shares of deceased owners.

SEC. 4. That the last clause of section fifty-two hundred and five of said statutes is hereby amended by adding to the said section the following proviso:

Sale of stock of shareholder refusing to pay assessment. See sec. 5205, p. 31.

"*And provided,* That if any shareholder or shareholders of such bank shall neglect or refuse, after three months' notice, to pay the assessment, as provided in this section, it shall be the duty of the board of directors to cause a sufficient amount of the capital stock of such shareholder or shareholders to be sold at public auction (after thirty days' notice shall be given by posting such notice of sale in the office of the bank, and by publishing such notice in a newspaper of the city or town in which the bank is located, or in a newspaper published nearest thereto,) to make good the deficiency; and the balance, if any, shall be returned to such delinquent shareholder or shareholders."

SEC. 5. That all United States officers charged with the receipt or disbursement of public moneys, and all officers of national banks shall stamp or write in plain letters the word "counterfeit" "altered" or "worthless," upon all fraudulent notes issued in the form of, and intended to circulate as money which shall be presented at their places of business; and if such officers shall wrongfully stamp any genuine note of the United States, or of the national banks, they shall, upon presentation, redeem such notes at the face-value thereof.

Disbursing and bank officers to stamp counterfeit notes.

SEC. 6. That all savings-banks or savings and trust companies organized under authority of any act of Congress shall be, and are hereby, required to make, to the Comptroller of the Currency, and publish, all the reports which national banking associations are required to make and publish under the provisions of sections fifty-two hundred and eleven, fifty-two hundred and twelve and fifty-two hundred and thirteen, of the Revised Statutes, and shall be subject to the same penalties for failure to make or publish such reports as are therein provided; which penalties may be collected by suit before any court of the United States in the district in which said savings banks or savings and trust companies may be located. And all savings or other banks now organized, or which shall hereafter be organized, in the District of Columbia, under any act of Congress, which shall have capital stock paid up in whole or in part, shall be subject to all the provisions of the Revised Statutes, and of all acts of Congress applicable to national banking-associations, so far as the same may be applicable to such savings or other banks: *Provided*, That such savings banks now established shall not be required to have a paid-in capital exceeding one hundred thousand dollars.

Savings-banks and trust companies to make and publish reports. See secs. 5211-5213, p. 32.

Savings and other banks in District of Columbia to be subject to national banking laws.

Approved, June 30, 1876.

AN ACT

Authorizing the conversion of national gold banks.

Be it enacted by the Senate and House of Representatives of the United States of America in Congress assembled, That any national gold bank organized under the provisions of the laws of the United States, may, in the manner and subject to the provisions prescribed by section fifty-one hun-

National gold banks may become currency banks.

Date of organization certificates

dred and fifty-four of the Revised Statutes of the United States, for the conversion of banks incorporated under the laws of any State, cease to be a gold bank, and become such an association as is authorized by section fifty-one hundred and thirty three, for carrying on the business of banking, and shall have the same powers and privileges, and shall be subject to the same duties, responsibilities, and rules, in all respects, as are by law prescribed for such associations: *Provided*, That all certificates of organization which shall be issued under this act shall bear the date of the original organization of each bank respectively as a gold bank.

Approved, February 14, 1880.

AN ACT

Defining the verification of returns of national banks.

Be it enacted by the Senate and House of Representatives of the United States of America in Congress assembled, That the oath or affirmation required by section fifty-two hundred and eleven of the Revised Statutes, verifying the returns made by national banks to the Comptroller of the Currency, when taken before a notary public properly authorized and commissioned by the State in which such notary resides and the bank is located, or any other officer having an official seal, authorized in such State to administer oaths, shall be a sufficient verification as contemplated by said section fifty-two hundred and eleven : *Provided*, That the officer administering the oath is not an officer of the bank.

Approved, February 26, 1881.

AN ACT

To enable national-banking associations to extend their corporate existence, and for other purposes.

Be it enacted by the Senate and House of Representatives of the United States of America in Congress assembled, That any national-banking association organized under the acts of February twenty-fifth, eighteen hundred and sixty-three,

June third, eighteen hundred and sixty-four, and February fourteenth, eighteen hundred and eighty, or under sections fifty-one hundred and thirty-three, fifty-one hundred and thirty-four, fifty-one hundred and thirty-five, fifty-one hundred and thirty-six, and fifty-one hundred and fifty-four of the Revised Statutes of the United States, may, at any time within the two years next previous to the date of the expiration of its corporate existence under present law, and with the approval of the Comptroller of the Currency, to be granted as hereinafter provided, extend its period of succession by amending its articles of association for a term of not more than twenty years from the expiration of the period of succession named in said articles of association, and shall have succession for such extended period, unless sooner dissolved by the act of shareholders owning two-thirds of its stock, or unless its franchise becomes forfeited by some violation of law, or unless hereafter modified or repealed.

Associations may extend period of succession for twenty years by amendment of articles of association.

Sec. 2. That such amendment of said articles of association shall be authorized by the consent in writing of shareholders owning not less than two-thirds of the capital stock of the association; and the board of directors shall cause such consent to be certified under the seal of the association, by its president or cashier, to the Comptroller of the Currency, accompanied by an application made by the president or cashier for the approval of the amended articles of association by the Comptroller; and such amended articles of association shall not be valid until the Comptroller shall give to such association a certificate under his hand and seal that the association has complied with all the provisions required to be complied with, and is authorized to have succession for the extended period named in the amended articles of association.

Amendment to be authorized by consent in writing of stockholders owning two-thirds of stock.

Certificate of Comptroller.

Sec. 3. That upon the receipt of the application and certificate of the association provided for in the preceding section, the Comptroller of the Currency shall cause a special examination to be made, at the expense of the association, to determine its condition; and if after such examination or otherwise it appears to him that said association is in a satisfactory condition, he shall grant his certificate of approval provided for in the preceding section, or if it appears that the condition of said association is not satisfactory, he shall withhold such certificate of approval.

Special examination to be made

Certificate of approval, when to be granted.

SEC. 4. That any association so extending the period of its succession shall continue to enjoy all the rights and privileges and immunities granted and shall continue to be subject to all the duties, liabilities, and restrictions imposed by the Revised Statutes of the United States and other acts having reference to national-banking associations, and it shall continue to be in all respects the identical association it was before the extension of its period of succession : *Provided, however,* That the jurisdiction for suits hereafter brought by or against any association established under any law providing for national-banking associations, except suits between them and the United States, or its officers and agents, shall be the same as, and not other than, the jurisdiction for suits by or against banks not organized under any law of the United States which do or might do banking business where such national-banking associations may be doing business when such suits may be begun. And all laws and parts of laws of the United States inconsistent with this proviso be, and the same are hereby, repealed.

Rights, privileges, immunities, liabilities, and restrictions of extended associations continued.

Jurisdiction of suits by and against national associations.

SEC. 5. That when any national-banking association has amended its articles of association as provided in this act, and the Comptroller has granted his certificate of approval, any shareholder not assenting to such amendment may give notice in writing to the directors, within thirty days from the date of the certificate of approval, of his desire to withdraw from said association, in which case he shall be entitled to receive from said banking association the value of the shares so held by him, to be ascertained by an appraisal made by a committee of three persons, one to be selected by such shareholder, one by the directors, and the third by the first two; and in case the value so fixed shall not be satisfactory to any such shareholder, he may appeal to the Comptroller of the Currency, who shall cause a reappraisal to be made, which shall be final and binding; and if said reappraisal shall exceed the value fixed by said committee, the bank shall pay the expenses of said reappraisal, and otherwise the appellant shall pay said expenses; and the value so ascertained and determined shall be deemed to be a debt due, and be forthwith paid, to said shareholder, from said bank; and the shares so surrendered and appraised shall, after due notice, be sold at public sale, within thirty days after the final appraisal provided in this section:

Shareholders not assenting to extension may give notice to directors.

Value of shares to be ascertained by appraisal.

When reappraisal may be made.

Provided, That in the organization of any banking associa- Associations in place of other associations, rights of shareholders. tion intented to replace any existing banking association, and retaining the name thereof, the holders of stock in the expiring association shall be entitled to preference in the allotment of the shares of the new association in proportion to the number of shares held by them respectively in the expiring association.

SEC. 6. That the circulating notes of any association so Circulating notes of extended associations to be redeemed at Treasury. extending the period of its succession which shall have been issued to it prior to such extension shall be redeemed at the Treasury of the United States, as provided in section three of the act of June twentith, eighteen hundred and seventy-four, entitled "An act fixing the amount of United States notes, providing for redistribution of national-bank currency, and for other purposes," and such notes when redeemed shall be forwarded to the Comptroller of the Currency, and destroyed, as now provided by law; and at the end of three years from the date of the extension of the corporate existence of each bank the association so extended Lawful money to be deposited after three years from date of extension. shall deposit lawful money with the Treasurer of the United States sufficient to redeem the remainder of the circulation which was outstanding at the date of its extension, as provided in sections fifty-two hundred and twenty-two, fifty-two hundred and twenty-four, and fifty-two hundred and twenty-five of the Revised Statutes; and any gain that may arise from the failure to present such circulating notes for redemption shall inure to the benefit of the United States; and from time to time, as such notes are redeemed or lawful New circulating notes with new devices to be issued. money deposited therefor as provided herein, new circulating notes shall be issued as provided for by this act, bearing such devices, to be approved by the Secretary of the Treasury, as shall make them readily distinguishable from the circulating notes heretofore issued: *Provided, however,* Each association to reimburse cost of plates. That each banking association which shall obtain the benefit of this act shall reimburse to the Treasury the cost of preparing the plate or plates for such new circulating notes as shall be issued to it.

SEC. 7. That national-banking associations whose corpo- Associations whose corporate existenc eexpires must act under sections 5220 and 5221 Rev. Stats., page 36. rate existence has expired or shall hereafter expire, and which do not avail themselves of the provisions of this act, shall be required to comply with the provisions of sections fifty-two hundred and twenty one and fifty-two hundred and twenty-two of the Revised Statutes in the same manner as if the shareholders had voted to go into liquidation, as provided in section fifty-two hundred and twenty of the Revised Statutes; and the provisions of sections fifty-two hundred and twenty-four and fifty-two hundred and twenty-five of the Revised Statutes shall also be applicable to such associations, except as modified by this act; and the franchise of such associations is hereby extended for the sole purpose of liquidating their affairs until such affairs are finally closed.

Also under sections 5224 and 5225.

Franchise extended for purposes of liquidation.

SEC. 8. That national banks now organized or hereafter organized, having a capital of one hundred and fifty thousand dollars or less, shall not be required to keep on deposit or deposit with the Treasurer of the United States United States bonds in excess of one-fourth of their capital stock as security for their circulating notes, but such banks shall keep on deposit or deposit with the Treasurer of the United States the amount of bonds as herein required; and such of those banks having on deposit bonds in excess of that amount are authorized to reduce their circulation by the deposit of lawful money as provided by law: *Provided,* That the amount of such circulating notes shall not exceed in any case ninety per centum of the par value of the bonds deposited as herein provided: *Provided further,* That the national banks which shall hereafter make deposits of lawful money for the retirement in full of their circulation shall, at the time of their deposit, be assessed, for the cost of transporting and redeeming their notes then outstanding, a sum equal to the average cost of the redemption of national-bank notes during the preceding year, and shall thereupon pay such assessment; and all national banks which have heretofore made or shall hereafter make deposits of lawful money for the reduction of their circulation, shall be assessed, and shall pay an assessment in the manner specified in section three of the act approved June twentieth, eighteen hundred and seventy-four, for the cost of transporting and redeeming their notes redeemed from such deposits subsequently to June thirtieth, eighteen hundred and eighty-one.

Associations with $150,000 capital or less may reduce bonds to ¼ capital.

Circulation not to exceed 90 per cent. of par value of bonds.

Association to be assessed for cost of transporting and redeeming notes.

SEC. 9. That any national-banking association now organized, or hereafter organized, desiring to withdraw its circulating notes, upon a deposit of lawful money with the Treasurer of the United States, as provided in section four of

Associations retiring circulation and withdrawing bonds cannot receive now circulation for six months.

the act of June twentieth, eighteen hundred and seventy-four, entitled "An act fixing the amount of United States notes, providing for a redistribution of national bank currency, and for other purposes," or as provided in this act, is authorized to deposit lawful money and withdraw a proportionate amount of the bonds held as security for its circulating notes in the order of such deposits; and no national bank which makes any deposit of lawful money in order to withdraw its circulating notes shall be entitled to receive any increase of its circulation for the period of six months from the time it made such deposit of lawful money for the purpose aforesaid: *Provided*, That not more than three millions of dollars of lawful money shall be deposited during any calendar month for this purpose: *And provided further*, That the provisions of this section shall not apply to bonds called for redemption by the Secretary of the Treasury, nor to the withdrawal of circulating notes in consequence thereof.

Not more than $3,000,000 in lawful money to be deposited in any calendar month except for called bonds.

SEC. 10. That upon a deposit of bonds as described by sections fifty-one hundred and fifty-nine and fifty-one hundred and sixty, except as modified by section four of an act entitled "An act fixing the amount of United States notes, providing for a redistribution of the national-bank currency, and for other purposes," approved June twentieth, eighteen hundred and seventy-four, and as modified by section eight of this act, the association making the same shall be entitled to receive from the Comptroller of the Currency circulating notes of different denominations, in blank, registered and countersigned as provided by law, equal in amount to ninety per centum of the current market value not exceeding par, of the United States bonds so transferred and delivered, and at no time shall the total amount of such notes issued to any such association exceed ninety per centum of the amount at such time actually paid in of its capital stock; and the provisions of sections fifty-one hundred and seventy-one and fifty-one hundred and seventy-six of the Revised Statutes are here hereby repealed.

Amount of circulation to be issued on U. S. bonds.

Proportion to capital; see also proviso in sec. 8, page 74.

Sections 5171 and 5176 repealed.

SEC. 11. That the Secretary of the Treasury is hereby authorized to receive at the Treasury any bonds of the United States bearing three and a half per centum interest, and to issue in exchange therefor an equal amount of registered bonds of the United States of the denominations of

Three and one-half per cent. bonds may be exchanged for threes.

fifty, one hundred, five hundred, one thousand, and ten thousand dollars, of such form as he may prescribe, bearing interest at the rate of three per centum per annum, payable quarterly at the Treasury of the United States. Such bonds shall be exempt from all taxation by or under State authority, and be payable at the pleasure of the United States: *Provided,* That the bonds herein authorized shall not be called in and paid so long as any bonds of the United States heretofore issued bearing a higher rate of interest than three per centum, and which shall be redeemable at the pleasure of the United States, shall be outstanding and uncalled. The last of the said bonds originally issued under this act, and their substitutes, shall be first called in, and this order of payment shall be followed until all shall have been paid.

SEC. 12. That the Secretary of the Treasury is authorized and directed to receive deposits of gold coin with the Treasurer or assistant treasurers of the United States, in sums not less than twenty dollars, and to issue certificates therefor in denominations of not less than twenty dollars each, corresponding with the denominations of United States notes. The coin deposited for or representing the certificates of deposit shall be retained in the Treasury for the payment of the same on demand. Said certificates shall be receivable for customs, taxes, and all public dues, and when so received may be reissued; and such certificates, as also silver certificates, when held by any national-banking association, shall be counted as part of its lawful reserve; and no national-banking association shall be a member of any clearing-house in which such certificates shall not be receivable in the settlement of clearing-house balances: *Provided,* That the Secretary of the Treasury shall suspend the issue of such gold certificates whenever the amount of gold coin and gold bullion in the Treasury reserved for the redemption of United States notes falls below one hundred millions of dollars; and the provisions of section fifty-two hundred and seven of the Revised Statutes shall be applicable to the certificates herein authorized and directed to be issued.

SEC. 13. That any officer, clerk, or agent of any national-banking association who shall wilfully violate the provisions of an act entitled "An act in reference to certifying checks by national banks," approved March third, eighteen hundred and sixty-nine, being section fifty-two hundred and eight of

Marginal notes: Three per cent. bonds exempt from taxation. Last issued to be called first. Secretary may issue gold certificates. Gold certificates receivable for customs, &c. Gold and silver certificates counted as reserve. Issue of gold certificates, when suspended. Certified checks not to be issued contrary to provisions of act March 3, 1869.

the Revised Statutes of the United States, or who shall resort to any device, or receive any fictitious obligation, direct or collateral, in order to evade the provisions thereof, or who shall certify checks before the amount thereof shall have been regularly entered to the credit of the dealer upon the books of the banking association, shall be deemed guilty of a misdemeanor, and shall, on conviction thereof in any circuit or district court of the United States, be fined not more than five thousand dollars, or shall be imprisoned not more than five years, or both, in the discretion of the court.

Penalty for illegal issue of certified checks.

SEC. 14. That Congress may at any time amend, alter, or repeal this act and the acts of which this is amendatory.

Approved July 12, 1882.

ACTS NOT OF A GENERAL NATURE.

1868-'82.

ACTS NOT OF A GENERAL NATURE.

AN ACT

Authorizing the First National Bank of Annapolis to change its location and name.

Be it enacted by the Senate and House of Representatives of the United States of America in Congress assembled, That the First National Bank of Annapolis, now located in the city of Annapolis, and State of Maryland, is hereby authorized to change its location to the city of Baltimore, in said State. Whenever the stockholders representing three-fourths of the capital of said bank, at a meeting called for that purpose, determine to make such change, the president and cashier shall execute a certificate, under the corporate seal of the bank, specifying such determination, and shall cause the same to be recorded in the office of the Comptroller of the Currency, and thereupon such change of location shall be effected, and the operations of discount and deposit of said bank shall be carried on in the city of Baltimore.

SEC. 2. That nothing in this act contained shall be so construed as in any manner to release the said bank from any liability or affect any action or proceeding in law in which the said bank may be a party or interested. And when such change shall have been determined upon, as aforesaid, notice thereof, and of such change, shall be published in two weekly papers in the city of Annapolis not less than four weeks.

SEC. 3. That whenever the location of said bank shall have been changed from the city of Annapolis to the city of Baltimore, in accordance with the first section of this act, its name shall be changed to The Traders' National Bank of Baltimore, if the board of directors of said bank shall accept the new name by resolution of the board, and cause a copy of such resolution, duly authenticated, to be filed with the Comptroller of the Currency.

SEC. 4. That all the debts, demands, liabilities, rights, privileges, and powers of the First National Bank of Annapolis shall devolve upon The Traders' National Bank of Baltimore, whenever such change of name is effected.

SEC. 5. That this act shall take effect and be in force from and after its passage.

Approved June 7, 1872.

2761——6 (81)

Acts of a similar nature to the one preceding have been enacted by Congress for the following purposes:

Authorizing The Manufacturers' National Bank of New York to change its location from the city of New York to the city of Brooklyn.
Approved July 27, 1868.

Authorizing The City National Bank of New Orleans, Louisiana, to change its name to The Germania National Bank of New Orleans.
Approved March 1, 1869.

Authorizing The Second National Bank of Plattsburgh, New York, to change its name to The Vilas National Bank of Plattsburgh.
Approved March 1, 1869.

Authorizing The First National Bank of Delhi, New York, to change its location and name to The First National Bank of Port Jervis, New York.
Approved May 5, 1870.

Authorizing The First National Bank of Fort Smith, Arkansas, to change its location and name to The First National Bank of Camden, Arkansas.
Approved July 1, 1870.

Authorizing The Jersey Shore National Bank, Pennsylvania, to change its location and name to The Williamsport National Bank, Pennsylvania.
Approved December 22, 1870.

Authorizing The Worcester County National Bank of Blackstone, Massachusetts, to change its location and name to The Franklin National Bank, Massachusetts.
Approved February 9, 1871.

Authorizing The Farmers' National Bank of Fort Edward, New York, to change its location and name to The North Granville National Bank, New York.
Approved February 18, 1871.

Authorizing The Worthington National Bank of Cooperstown, New York, to change its location and name to The First National Bank of Oneonta, New York.
Approved February 27, 1871.

Authorizing The Warren National Bank of South Danvers, Massachusetts, to change its name to The Warren National Bank of Peabody, Massachusetts.

Approved March 12, 1872.

Authorizing The First National Bank of Seneca, Illinois, to change its location and name to The First National Bank of Morris, Illinois. (Two acts.)

Approved April 5, 1872, and June 18, 1874.

Authorizing The Railroad National Bank of Lowell, Massachusetts, to change its location and name to The Railroad National Bank of Boston, Massachusetts.

Approved May 31, 1872.

Authorizing The National Bank of Lyons, Michigan, to change its location and name to The Second National Bank of Ionia, Michigan.

Approved December 24, 1872.

Authorizing The East Chester National Bank of Mount Vernon, New York, to change its location and name to The German National Bank of Evansville, Indiana.

Approved January 11, 1873.

Authorizing The First National Bank of Newnan, Georgia, to change its location and name to The National Bank of Commerce, Atlanta, Georgia.

Approved January 23, 1873.

Authorizing The First National Bank of Watkins, New York, to change its location and name to The First National Bank of Penn Yan, New York.

Approved February 19, 1873.

Authorizing The National Bank of Springfield, Missouri, to change its name to The First National Bank of Springfield, Missouri.

Approved March 3, 1873.

Authorizing The Kansas Valley National Bank of Topeka, Kansas, to change its name to The First National Bank of Topeka, Kansas.

Approved March 3, 1873.

Authorizing The First National Bank of Saint Anthony, Minnesota, to change its location and name to The Merchants' National Bank of Minneapolis, Minnesota.

Approved January 8, 1874.

Authorizing The Second National Bank of Havana, New York, to change its name to The Havana National Bank of Havana, New York.

Approved January 9, 1874.

Authorizing The Passaic County National Bank of Paterson, New Jersey, to change its name to The Second National Bank of Paterson, New Jersey.

Approved April 15, 1874.

Authorizing The Citizens' National Bank of Hagerstown, Maryland, to change its location and name to The Citizens' National Bank of Washington City, District of Columbia.

Approved May 1, 1874.

Authorizing The Irasburg National Bank of Orleans, at Irasburg, Vermont, to change its location and name to The Barton National Bank, Vermont.

Approved June 3, 1874.

Authorizing The Farmers' National Bank of Greensburg, Pennsylvania, to change its location and name to The Fifth National Bank of Pittsburgh, Pennsylvania.

Approved June 23, 1874.

Authorizing The Citizens' National Bank of Sanbornton, New Hampshire, to change its name to The Citizens' National Bank of Tilton, New Hampshire.

Approved February 19, 1875.

Authorizing The Second National Bank of Jamestown, New York, to change its name to The City National Bank of Jamestown, New York.

Approved March 3, 1875.

Authorizing The Second National Bank of Watkins, New York, to change its name to The Watkins National Bank, New York.

Approved March 3, 1875.

Authorizing The Slater National Bank of North Providence, Rhode Island, to change its name to The Slater National Bank of Pawtucket, Rhode Island.

Approved March 3, 1875.

Authorizing The Auburn City National Bank of Auburn, New York, to be consolidated with The First National Bank of Auburn, New York.

Approved March 3, 1875.

Authorizing The Miners' National Bank of Braidwood, Illinois, to change its location and name to The Commercial National Bank of Wilmington, Illinois.

Approved January 31, 1878.

Authorizing The Windham National Bank, Windham, Connecticut, to change its location to the village of Willimantic, Connecticut.

Approved February 10, 1879.

Authorizing The National Bank of Commerce of Cincinnati, Ohio, to change its name to The National Lafayette and Bank of Commerce.

Approved April 29, 1879.

Authorizing The City National Bank of Manchester, New Hampshire, to change its name to The Merchants' National Bank of Manchester.

Approved June 11, 1880.

Authorizing The Blue Hill National Bank of Dorchester, Massachusetts, to change its location and name to The Blue Hill National Bank of Milton, Massachusetts.

Approved January 13, 1881.

Authorizing The First National Bank of Meriden, West Meriden, Connecticut, to change its name to The First National Bank of Meriden, Meriden, Connecticut.

Approved March 1, 1881.

Authorizing The National Mechanics' Banking Association of New York, New York, to change its name to Wall Street National Bank.

Approved February 14, 1882.

Authorizing The Lancaster National Bank of Lancaster, Massachusetts, to change its location and name to The Lancaster National Bank of Clinton, Clinton, Massachusetts.

Approved February 25, 1882.

Authorizing The National Bank of Kutztown, Pennsylvania, to change its location and name to The Keystone National Bank of Reading, Pennsylvania. .

Approved June 27, 1882.

INDEX.

A.

(87)

88

89

90

93

2761——7

98

O.

106

109

2761——8

U.

V.

W.

116